THE LIGHT HORSE BREEDS

Ace O' Goshen

THE LIGHT HORSE BREEDS

THEIR ORIGIN, CHARACTERISTICS, AND PRINCIPAL USES

by John W. Patten

A. S. BARNES & COMPANY, INC. • NEW YORK
THOMAS YOSELOFF LTD. • LONDON

Library of Congress Catalog Card Number: 59-12547

A. S. Barnes and Company, Inc.
11 East 36th Street
New York 16, N. Y.

Thomas Yoseloff Ltd.
123 New Bond Street
London, W.1, England

Printed in the United States of America

Appreciation

In preparing this outline of the origin, characteristics, and principal uses of the fifteen primary breeds, and also the data on the United States Equestrian Team, the author has received the cooperation of their respective organizations or journals. Their assistance is gratefully acknowledged.

A large number of the pictures herein were loaned by the owners or by the several breeds' associations, clubs, or societies, or their respective journals. Their cooperation and graciousness are much appreciated.

J. W. P.

Preface

The origin, characteristics, and principal uses of fifteen primary light horse and miniature breeds are outlined herein, including data on the United States Equestrian Team, each supplemented by representative pictures. In addition, a Gallery of Miscellany is presented of Horse Shows and the like, Jumping, Polo Playing, Pony Harness Racing, Youthful Competitors, and Various—Unusual.

There are over 300 pictures, of some 29 light horse and miniature breeds from all parts of the United States, Arabia, Argentina, Austria, Canada, Cuba, England, France, Germany, Ireland, Italy, Mexico, New Zealand, Russia, Scotland, Wales, and the Scandinavian countries: Denmark, Iceland, Norway, and Sweden.

A number of readers may be interested in the first known horse, "The Dawn Horse." A note concerning it is included in an Introduction.

JOHN W. PATTEN

Contents

Illustrations

Appaloosa

Broodmares and Foals, Mr. George B. Hatley
Chief of Fourmile
Rustler Bill
Simcoe's Sarcee
Toby II

Arab

Alyfar
Ata Aia
Al-Marah Radames
Al-Marah Rooz
Al-Marah Rose Anne
Bint Rihani
Broodmares and Foals, Joder Arabian Farm
Broodmares and Foals and Stallion, Jordan Arabian Farm
Casanova
El Chazaam
El Rahnason
Ibn Rogue
Indraff
Jordan
Rakiz
Rasan
Imp. Rose Marie and Foal
Roseana
Stardai
Starrdana
Zab and Al-Marah El Hezzez, Pair

Connemara

Imp. Lystra Lad
Squire and Little Squire, Pair
Whitewood Biscuit
Whitewood Cornpone
Imp. Wicklow Mountain Rose Bay

Hackney

> *Cassilis Glen Ideal*
> *Cassilis Minuet*
> *Cassilis Sir Echo*
> *Cassilis Viceroy and Minaret of Hillingdon, Pair*
> *Cora's Mite*
> *Dream of Hillingdon*
> *Echo of Hillingdon and Dream of Hillingdon, Tandem*
> *Karen*
> *Minaret of Hillingdon*
> *Red Letter*
> *Whippoorwill Masterpiece*

Morgan

> *Broodmares and Foals, Richard's Ranch*
> *Lippitt Mandate*
> *Little Miss Pepper*
> *Nancy Ann*
> *Red (Morgan-Arab)*
> *Windcrest Donfield*
> *Windcrest Sentimental Lady*

Palomino

> *Catoctin Gold*
> *Golden Belle*
> *Top Hat*

Pinto

Overo Type
> *Dor's Black Victory*

Morocco Type
> *Kanhwa*

Tobiano Type
> *Baby Doll*
> *Flicka*
> *Flying Kite*
> *Lady Rose and Silver Dawn, Pair*
> *Trigger*

Quarter Horse
  Caillet's King
  Cricket Dowdy
  Joe Queen
  King's Joe Boy
  Wig and Foal

Shetland Pony
  Carolanne Farm Pony Hitch
  Curtiss Friscoe Pete
  Dainty Doll
  Silver Mane's Meteor Cody

Harness Racing
  Silver Smoke
  Susie's Miss Boots

Tennessee Walking Horse
  Go Boy's Ace
  Go Boy's Souvenir
  Merry Go Boy
  Midnight Mystery
  Sun's Big Shot

Welsh Mountain Pony
  Brierwood Honey
  Coed Coch Meilyr
  Imp. Coed Coch Pelen and Foal
  Coed Coch Siaradus and Foal
  Imp. Farnley Sirius
  Gretton Sunbeam
  Gretton Sunlight
  Liseter Bright Light
  Liseter Shooting Star

Standardbred
  Trotters
        Emily's Pride, (3) 1:58
        Galophone, 1:58 1/5
        Greyhound, 1:55 1/4
        Greyhound, 2:01 3/4—Under Saddle
        Hickory Pride, (3), 2:01 2/5
        Hickory Smoke, (3) 1:58 2/5
        Novelle Hanover and Twin Foals by Galophone, 1:58 1/5
        Rosalind, 1:56 3/4
        Greyhound and Rosalind, 1:58 1/4—to Pole
        Star's Pride, 1:57 1/5
        Titan Hanover, (3) 1:58

  Pacers
        Billy Direct, 1:55
        Dan Patch, 1:55 1/4
        Her Ladyship, 1:56 3/4
        Hollyrood Volo, 2:00 1/4
        Meadow War, 2:02 2/5
        Van Hanover, (3) 2:02 3/5
  Harness Racing
    United States
        Countess Adios
        DuQuoin State Fair Track, DuQuoin, Illinois
        Hairos, Crevalcore, and Silver Song
        Historic Track, Goshen, New York
        Saratoga Raceway, Saratoga Springs, New York
    Scandinavian Tracks
        Charlottelund Track, Charlottelund, Denmark
        Bjerkebänen Track, Oslo, Norway
        Solvälla Track, Stockholm, Sweden

Thoroughbred
        Bold Ruler
        Citation
        Uncle Miltie

A Quartet of Champions
  Capot, Coaltown, Nashua, and Tom Fool
Thoroughbred Racing
  United States
    The New York Racing Association, Inc.
      Aqueduct Race Course, Aqueduct, New York
      Belmont Park Race Course, Elmont, New York
      Saratoga Race Course, Saratoga Springs, New York
    Monmouth Park Race Course, Oceanport, New Jersey
    Gulf Stream Race Course, Hallandale, Florida
    Hialeah Race Course, Hialeah, Florida
    Washington, D.C., International Race
      Laurel Race Course, Laurel, Maryland
  Cuba
    Oriental Park Race Course, Havana (Marianao), Cuba

United States Equestrian Team
    *Mr. George Morris, Member, Mr. Bertalan de Nemethy,
      Coach, and Mr. Frank Chapot, Member*
    *Mr. Wm. C. Steinkraus, Captain, Mr. George Morris
      and Mr. Hugh Wiley, Members, and "Nautical"*
    *"Master William," Mr. Hugh Wiley, Member, and
      "Nautical"*
    Defense, Mr. Frank Chapot Up
    Ksar d'Esprit, Mr. Wm. C. Steinkraus Up
    Master William, Mr. Hugh Wiley Up
    Sinjon, Mr. George Morris Up

  Jumping Arenas
    *Pennsylvania National Horse Show, State Farm Show Build-
      ing Arena, Harrisburg, Pennsylvania*
    *New York National Horse Show, Madison Square Garden,
      New York, New York*

A Gallery of Miscellany
  Horse Shows, Etc.
    Bellwood Horse Show Ring, Bellwood, Pennsylvania

THE LIGHT HORSE BREEDS

Introduction

The first horse was the Dawn Horse (*eohippus*), one of the mammalia that inhabited the earth at the dawn of the age of mammals, following the dinosaur age. *Eohippus* is derived from *eo,* a Greek combining form meaning dawn, and *hippus,* the Greek word for horse, thus Dawn Horse.

That horses inhabited the earth millions of years ago is evidenced by fossil discoveries by scientific expeditions in many parts of the world, including our own states of New Mexico and Wyoming.

Scientists have determined several interesting and historically useful things about the early horses; among them are the following:

1. They once lived in North America, and then disappeared until returned by man many thousands of years later.
2. They were originally of small sizes, varying from eighteen inches to twenty-four inches in height and from eighty pounds to one hundred twenty pounds in weight.
3. They lived on grasses and foliage.
4. They were split-toed, with four toes on the front feet and three on the hind feet, and the middle toe of each foot was considerably larger than the others.
5. They apparently used their middle toes much more than the others, particularly when running. The weight was then borne by the middle toes and, through the years, these toes became larger and stronger, with the other toes disappearing, and a solid-footed equine evolved.

During the era of the Dawn Horses, North America was connected by land to Asia. Whether the Dawn Horse originated in what is now known as North America and went overland to Asia and Africa or vice versa is beyond the concept of this writing. It is sufficient here to mention their physical existence and form millions of years ago and hasten to modern eras when horses, either in their natural habitat by natural selection or by man's selective breeding, developed many different types and breeds of horses and ponies.

The Romans were the first to classify the movements of horses according to their action (gait) and use (work). Here we are interested in the light and miniature breeds. The two actions of special interest identified and classified by the Romans are first the trot (*stinerarii*) and second the amble or pace (*ambulaturarii*).

We also are especially interested here in the primary light horse and miniature breeds from approximately the fifteenth century to the present.

Christopher Columbus, when he landed in the West Indies in 1492, was known to have brought five mares and twenty stallions. These horses descended from Barbs, war horses used by the Moors in the invasion of Spain in 710. Later Spanish colonists arrived in the West Indies with many types and sizes of the then existing Spanish horses. Cortez, when he sailed from Cuba to Mexico in 1519, took along some twenty horses, previously brought from Spain. Later thousands more were sent direct to him from Spain to aid in conquering the Aztecs. De Soto brought several hundred horses to Florida in 1539. Many of these were used on the exploratory expedition westward that resulted in the discovery of the Mississippi River. From these several groups of horses, many escaped and many were freed (turned loose); they eventually intermingled with other groups and moved freely throughout the South, Southwest, and West.

These admixtures, the mares especially, became the native horses from which, by crossing with horses from other countries (principally via England), a number of breeds evolved in North America.

The several breeds developed in North America are: American Albino, American Saddlebred, Appaloosa, Morgan, Palomino, Pinto, Quarter Horse, Standardbred Trotter and Pacer, and Tennessee Walking. In addition, the following breeds developed in the British Isles now have established lines in this country: Hackney Horse, Thoroughbred Horse, Connemara, Shetland Pony, and Welsh Pony.

White Wings, Stallion
Sire: Snowchief II

Dam: Lady Esther
By: Ambrose

White Horse Ranch, Mr. and Mrs. Caleb R. Thompson, Naper, Nebraska.

American Albino

Obedience

Owner: White Horse Ranch, Mr. and Mrs. Caleb R. Thompson, Naper, Nebraska.

American Albino

Origin

PLACE OF ORIGIN: United States; White Horse Ranch, Naper, Nebraska.

FOUNDATION: The foundation sire was Old King, a milk-white stallion, with pinkish skin and brown eyes, whose sire and dam were of untraced breeding, but believed to be predominantly Arab through his sire and Morgan through his dam evidenced by the carriage, coloring (Arab), conformation, expression, finish, strength, and style dominant in those two breeds.

Old King was of medium size with a beautifully formed head, wide-set lustrous eyes, and medium-length sharp-pointed ears, well-muscled neck and shoulders on a well-proportioned, rounded body, with a medium-short back, slightly rounded haunches tapering from the croup to the tail, set on medium-size flat-boned legs with long sloping pasterns, which were set on well-formed and concave feet with whitish or grayish hoofs. His mane and tail were white with long, fine, soft, and silky hairs.

The foundation mares were Morgan or of blood lines predominantly of the Morgan breed. To the cover of Old King those mares and other local native mares of quality invariably produced milk-white-haired, pinkish-skinned foals with either blue, brown, or hazel eyes—the image of their sire.

The development of a milk-white, pink-skinned, blue-, brown-, or hazel-eyed horse is attributable to the phenomenon of atavism. Atavism may be defined as a recurrence in an organism, or in any of its parts, of a form typical of ancestors more remote than parents; it is usually due to recombination of ancestral genes. An atavist is one that undergoes atavism: a throwback or reversion to ancestors more remote than parents.

Characteristics

COLORING: Milky-white hair, underlying pinkish skin, with blue, brown, or hazel eyes.

SIZE: Height varying from fourteen (14.0) hands to sixteen (16.0) hands. Weight varies from 1,000 pounds to 1,200 pounds.

In recent years pony mares of registered miniature breeding and of mixed breeding have been bred (crossed) to registered Albino stallions; the offspring are invariably milk-white haired and pinkish skinned, with either blue, brown, or hazel eyes. The foals mature to a top height of forty-eight inches (36 to 48 inches) and a top weight of five hundred pounds (250 to 500 pounds). Technically, they are small horses because they have not been segregated and classified separately by the American Albino Horse Club in its *Registry*, nor has a separate *Registry* (*Stud Book*) been established for them.

Other Characteristics

Exceptionally docile, smart, and tractable. Easy to teach their performances and routines, and once they are learned the Albinos retain them through their exceedingly long useful life.

Principal Uses

Showing under saddle, as parade mounts, and for general riding purposes. They are particularly noted—in fact are famous—as exhibition and circus performers: jumping singly and in pairs; two, three, four, five, and six abreast; and tandems of two, two pair (fours), and three pair (sixes), often with only one rider (a girl) handling them six abreast or in three-pair tandems. They jump obstacles and jump through fire without riders, also pyramid and perform other feats requiring a high degree of intelligence, training, execution, and obedience.

Registry

The American Albino Horse Club, Naper, Nebraska.

Cal Thompson, Founder

A Sextet

White Horse Ranch, Mr. and Mrs. Caleb R. Thompson, Naper, Nebraska.

Ten and Ten

Silver Slipper, Mare
Sire: Snowchief II

White Horse Ranch, Mr. and Mrs. Caleb R. Thompson, Naper, Nebraska.

Watering

White Wings, Horse   Rider: Mr. Caleb R. Thompson
Sire: Snowchief II

Owner: White Horse Ranch, Mr. and Mrs. Caleb R. Thompson, Naper, Nebraska.

Six Abreast

A Tandem of Six

White Horse Ranch, Mr. and Mrs. Caleb R. Thompson, Naper, Nebraska.

I Can Do It

Taking a Bow

Owner: White Horse Ranch, Mr. and Mrs. Caleb R. Thompson, Naper, Nebraska.

Ruth Thompson, Manager

Weanlings

Broodmares and Foals

White Horse Ranch, Mr. and Mrs. Caleb R. Thompson, Naper, Nebraska.

Special Assignment, Stallion
  Sire: Society Rex

Dam: Quaker Bonnett
  By: Kingston's Choice

In service: Minton Hickory Farm, Miss Nola Minton, Barbourville, Kentucky.

American Saddlebred

Whos Who, Colt (Weanling)
Sire: Ace O'Goshen

Owner: Robin Hill Stables, Mr. and Mrs. Fred M. Link, Westwood, New Jersey.

American Saddlebred

Origin

PLACE OF ORIGIN: United States, principally Fayette County, Kentucky.

FOUNDATION: The foundation stallions were of variable and mixed breeding. A Committee of The American Saddle Horse Breeders' Association applied itself for some ten years in revising and redetermining the foundation stock. Its recommendations were formally accepted by the Association at a meeting of the stockholders in April 1902.

A listing of the foundation stallions appears in Volume IV of the *American Saddle Horse Breeders' Association Stud Book*, p. XVII, as recommended by the Committee and approved by the Association. The following list as revised is arranged alphabetically: 1. Cabell's Lexington by Gist's Black Hawk (Morgan); 2. Pat Cleburne by Benton's Gray Diomed (Thoroughbred); 3. Coleman's Eureka (Thoroughbred-Morgan); 4. Davy Crockett; 5. Denmark (Thoroughbred) by Imp. Hedgeford; 6. John Dillard by Canadian Chief (Canadian); 7. Peter's Halcorn; 8. Stump-the-Dealer (Thoroughbred); 9. Tom Hal (imported from Canada); 10. Van Meter's Waxy (Thoroughbred). At a meeting of the Association on April 10, 1908, it was voted to designate Denmark as the sole foundation sire. This was done because of the great number of his registered descendants. The others were given numbers and placed on the Noted Deceased Sire List.

NOTE: The breeding of John Dillard and Tom Hal is not indicated; however, they are of a strain of pacing horses originating in Canada, imported to Rhode Island, and became known as Narragansett Pacers. They are to a considerable degree responsible for the stepping pace and the rack, two of the five gaits of American Saddlebred horses.

There are many great performers within the American Saddle Horse breed. One hardly dares to make a listing thereof, because so many immediately appear in vision. The stallions: Ace O'Goshen, American Born, Anacacho Shamrock, Bourbon King, Chief of Longview, Edna Mays' King, King's Genius, My Major Dare, and Rex McDonald; the mares: Alice Knight, America Beautiful, Belle of the Dell, Edith Fable, Flirtation Walk, Hazel Dawn, Roxie Highland, and Sweetheart on Parade; the geldings: John Barrymore, Johnny Jones, Storm Cloud, The Lemon Drop Kid, and many, many others and, not to be omitted, that rugged performer, stallion champion, and now great progenitor Wing Commander.

Characteristics

COLOR: Bay, black, brown, chestnut, golden, and gray. The chestnuts often have white markings and white legs. Gaudy white markings are not encouraged.

SIZE: Height varies from fourteen (14.0) hands to sixteen (16.0) hands. Weight varies from 900 pounds to 1,200 pounds.

OTHER CHARACTERISTICS: They are three-gaited and five-gaited. The three gaits are walk, trot, and canter. The five gaits are walk, trot, stepping pace, rack, and canter. Of the five gaits, the third, the stepping pace (modified pace), is referred to as the slow gait, as the beat is of slow tempo. The fourth, the rack (single foot), is called the fast gait, as the beat is of rapid tempo. The fifth, the canter, is referred to as a rocking chair gait, because it has rocking-chair characteristics and tempo. These three are easy riding gaits (easy and comfortable to the rider). The stepping pace and the canter are fairly easy on the horses but the rack is a somewhat exhausting gait, because of the speed with which it is executed. In bygone days the third gait was a fox trot, a slow, short, broken-type trot. It was executed with each hind foot striking the ground an instant before the diagonal front foot.

The stepping pace is a modified pace but the two legs on each side are not in simultaneous forward motion as in a true pace. It is a four-beat gait with each foot striking the ground separately at irregular intervals.

The rack is a brilliant, flashy, and fast four-beat gait with each foot striking the ground separately, at regular intervals.

The canter is a slow restrained gallop. It is a three-beat gait with the leading front foot and the diagonal hind foot absorbing a greater portion of the ground impact: hence the lead should frequently be changed. Within a fenced area or a circular arena the lead is some-what as the movement of a clock: when moving clockwise a right foot lead; moving counterclockwise, a left foot lead.

The breed is famous for its conformation: well-rounded short-coupled bodies, sound legs and feet, long graceful high-arched necks, high-set and flowing tails, the latter especially applicable to the five-gaiters. It is one of the most animated, beautiful, bold-going, fiery, and spirited breeds extant.

Principal Uses

Showing under saddle at three gaits and five gaits and in harness in fine harness classes, also under saddle and in harness in combination classes. Rarely shown in harness in pairs or multiple hitches.

The five-gaited horses are extensively used on plantations because of their easy riding gaits. Both gaits are used for pleasure riding and many successfully compete as high jumpers.

Registry

American Saddle Horse Breeders' Association, 929 South Fourth Street, Louisville, Kentucky.

Rona's Beau, Gelding   Driver: Mrs. Hertha C. Meyer

Owner: Mrs. Hertha C. Meyer, Walter Siefert Stables, Wayne, New Jersey.

Flirtation Walk, Mare
   Sire: King's Genius

Dam: Spelling Bee
   Rider: Charles Dunn

Wing Commander, Horse
   Sire: Anacacho Shamrock

Dam: Flirtation Walk
   By: King's Genius

Rider: Earl Teater

Owner: Dodge Stables, Mr. and Mrs. F. L. Van Lennep, Lexington, Kentucky.

King's Genius, Stallion   Dam: Princess Eugenia
    Sire: Bourbon King

    Owner: Walnut Springs Farm, Mr. Clifford Mooers, Houston, Texas.

Lady Carrigan, Mare   Dam: Mountain Raven
    Sire: Society Rex   Rider: Garland Bradshaw

    Owner: Broadland Stables, Miss Jolie Richardson, Atlanta, Georgia.

Dangerous Beau, Colt (2)
Sire: Beau Gallant

Storm O'Lee, Colt (1)
Sire: King of Rose-A-Lee

Owner: Shamrock Farm, Mr. Charles J. Cronan, Jr., Louisville, Kentucky.

Knight's Treasure, Mare
Sire: Gallant Knight

Rider: Charles Huston

Owner: Delaine Farm, Mr. Hubert S. Silberman, Morton Grove, Illinois.

Belle of The Dell, Mare
Sire: King Coe

Rider: Earl Teater

Owner: Dodge Stables, Mr. and Mrs. F. L. Van Lennep, Lexington, Kentucky.

Meadow Princess, Mare
Sire: Abie's Genius

Rider: Earl Teater

Sparkling Delight, Mare
Sire: Sparkling Waters

Rider: Miss Judy Johnson

Dodge Stables, Mr. and Mrs. F. L. Van Lennep, Lexington, Kentucky.

Delaine Sensation, Gelding   Driver: Mr. Hubert S. Silberman

Owner: Delaine Farm, Mr. Hubert S. Silberman, Morton Grove, Illinois.

Parading Lady, Mare   Driver: Mrs. Josephine Robinson

Owner: Mrs. Josephine Robinson, Versailles, Kentucky.

The Lemon Drop Kid, Gelding   Driver: Robert A. McCray
Owner: Sunnyslope Farms, Mr. R. B. Christy, Scott City, Kansas.

Easter Sunday, Gelding   Driver: Mrs. George M. Brewster
Owner: Holiday Farm, Mr. and Mrs. George M. Brewster, River Vale, New Jersey.

Wild Sensation, Gelding   Driver: Mrs. Bruce H. Seabright

Owner: Wakitatina Farms, Mr. Bruce H. Seabright, Bridgeport, Ohio.

Anacacho Shamrock, Stallion   Dam: Sally Cameron
Sire: Edna May's King   By: Highland's Squirrel King

Dodge Stables, Mr. and Mrs. F. L. Van Lennep, Lexington, Kentucky.

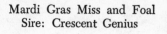

Mardi Gras Miss and Foal
Sire: Crescent Genius

Owner: Robin Hill Stables,
Mr. and Mrs. Fred M. Link, Westwood, New Jersey.

Alice Knight, Mare
Sire: Gallant Knight

Rider: Miss Daryl Link

Simcoe's Sarcee, Stallion   Dam: Morgan's Cheeta
   Sire: Simcoe's Chinook   By: Leopard Cortez

Owner: Mr. Charley W. Peterson, Atkinson, Nebraska.

Appaloosa

Toby II, Horse   Rider: Miss Patti Murphy
    Sire: Toby

Owner: Mr. George B. Hatley, Moscow, Idaho.

Appaloosa

Origin

PLACE OF ORIGIN: United States, principally in the northwestern states, from animals originating in Feranga, Central Asia. Mexico and several South American countries have a goodly number of the breed.

FOUNDATION: Horses now called Appaloosas appear in Chinese art dating to 500 B.C. and in Persian art of the fourteenth century. From Asia, by importation or by conquest, they arrived in Spain and her countries during the fourteenth and fifteenth centuries. Cortez brought a goodly number to North America when he invaded Mexico early in the sixteenth century.

Unlike the small-sized horse (Indian pony), the Appaloosa was a full-sized, well-turned, light horse when the Lewis and Clark expedition pierced the Northwest. They were held in considerable numbers by the Nez Percé tribe, inhabitants of an area that is now portions of the states of Idaho, Oregon, and Washington.

The name Appaloosa is derived from the Palouse country, a fertile area drained by the Palouse River. The colorful horses bred by the natives there were first called Palouse horses or, in local jargon, a Palouse. In later slurring, it became Apalouse, then Apalouser, and finally, Appaloosa.

Astute horsemen by selective breeding have developed Appaloosas into a dominant, consistent breed, recognized as such by the National Association of Stallion Registration Boards in 1950.

Characteristics

COLOR: Particolored skins are of grayish, brownish, dark bluish, and roanish backgrounds. Many are mottled in varying degrees and areas. The mottled skin is always evident around the genitalia. A white sclera always encircles the eyes. Many have wispy manes and sparse tails; in many the tails are stumpish and they are referred to variously as finger-tailed or rat-tailed. Varnish marks (dark areas) are common in the marbled pattern in those of roan coloration, on the nose, face (above the eyes), on the point of the hip, behind the elbow, and in the gaskin and stifle regions.

Just as many other breeds have different colors, the Appaloosa has different colors, and also different color patterns; actually, there are six basic patterns and another classed as marginal. It is somewhat lacking, or showing only a trace of Appaloosa coloring. The physical characteristics of the breed must be exceptionally strong, otherwise such an animal is not acceptable for registration. The basic color patterns are: 1. Frost; 2. Leopard; 3. Marble; 4. Snowflake; 5. Spotted Blanket; 6. White Blanket. Color is always desired in the breed, but not at the sacrifice of the horse. In addition, the hoofs of many show vertical stripes or laminations of black and white, running from the coronary band areas to the tip of the toes.

In transmission, the color patterns may vary; e.g., a spotted blanket mare bred to a snowflake stallion may foal a white blanket colt. Some colts when foaled do not have a distinctive coloring and pattern but as they mature one of the basic patterns develops, unless in rare cases a marginal results. The males tend toward more brilliant coloring than the females, as is common in wildlife and fowl. Certainly the Appaloosa breed with its multitudinous colorings is a fertile field of study for geneticists.

SIZES: Heights vary from fourteen two (14.2) hands to fifteen three (15.3) hands. Weights vary from 950 pounds to 1,275 pounds.

OTHER CHARACTERISTICS: Appaloosas have a high degree of endurance, energy, ruggedness, and spirit. They are tractable, easily trained and handled. Some are inclined to be "offish" to strangers, but once friends are made they are docile, welcome attention, and are perfectly trustworthy, in or out of the stable.

They are one of the larger light horse breeds; however, that does not handicap or impede them in the quickness necessary to stock handling, at which they serve admirably well.

Principal Uses

Stock handling; cutting, herding, roping, range-riding, and the like. Show and rodeo competition classes; cutting, working cow horses, reining, hazing, and the like. Endurance trials, parade mounts, police mounts, and also pleasure riding, generally under Western tack.

Registry

The Appaloosa Horse Club, Inc., Moscow, Idaho.

Broodmares and Foals

Owner: Mr. George B. Hatley, Moscow, Idaho.

Chief of Fourmile, Horse   Rider: William Pearson
    Sire: Piccolo

Chief of Fourmile, Stallion   Dam: Trixie
    Sire: Piccolo   By: Not Furnished

Owner: Mr. and Mrs. Gus Ottermann, San Antonio, Texas.

Rustler Bill, Horse
Sire: A Quarter Horse

Rider: Mr. Tom Aull

Rustler Bill, Stallion
Sire: A Quarter Horse

Dam and Sire: Appaloosa

Owner: Mr. Tom Aull, Aspermont, Texas.

El Rahnason, Stallion   Dam: Amaana
Sire: El Rahna   By: Jadaan

Owner: Gilbert and Pearl Larson, Sunnymead, California.

Arab

El Chazaam, Horse   Rider: Don Wardle
    Sire: Ghazamar

Owner: Dr. LaPrele Williams, Downey, California.

Arab

Origin

PLACE OF ORIGIN: Arabia and Egypt, especially the former, in the provinces of Nejd and Mesopotamia.

FOUNDATION: The Arab breed is of great antiquity; about its geographic origin there is dispute. Its presence in Arabia for twenty or more centuries among the Bedouin tribes of the Anazeh, Roala, Sebaa, and Shammar is well documented. They are a distinct subspecies of equines, having characteristics varying from other breeds. These differences appear in the conformation of the frame or skeleton and in intelligence and spotlight the Arab wherever the breed is found.

In his natural habitat the Arab was and is bred and raised in close proximity to and association with people. In such closeness of contact with humans, the breed developed a keenness of brain similar to the primitive dog. He served his people in conquest and war but most especially as a means of transportation and most particularly as an affectionate friend and companion. The breed is often referred to as Arabian. Technically, it is incorrect as the breed is *Arab* and the animals (horses) of the breed are *Arabians*.

Arabians have been exported to every part of the world, especially the males (stallions); these became and are the progenitor-founders of practically all the light horse and miniature breeds extant; specifically, without a complete listing, 1. Connemara, Ireland and America; 2. French Trotter, France; 3. Hackney, England and America; 4. Morgan, America; 5. Orloff Trotter, Russia; 6. Quarter Horse, America; 7. Saddlebred, America; 8. Standardbred, America; 9. Thoroughbred, England and elsewhere; 10. Welsh Pony, England and America.

Characteristics

COLOR: Bay, black (rarely), brown, chestnut, gray, and pure white (rarely). In their later years, when grays turn to white, they still at a distance appear to be grays, because the breed's black skin filters through. Stars, stripe and blaze faces, snip noses, and white stockings are common markings, especially in those of chestnut colorings.

SIZE: Height varies from fourteen (14.0) hands to fifteen two (15.2) hands. A few have reached sixteen (16.0) hands. In the future, sixteen hands (or nearly so) may become a common height in America by reason of the growing methods of their breeders: "a full feed trough and hay manger from infancy."

Weight varies from 800 pounds to 1,100 pounds; some males in the stud (stallions) reach 1,200 pounds.

As the Arab breed has been predominant in the foundation of other breeds, his physical structure should be described.

He has a relative shortness of skull, a slenderness of lower face, larger brain area (case), one less lumbar vertebra, and several less vertebrae in the tail bone and a more horizontal position of the pelvic bone than other breeds.

The head, at the upper half, is larger in proportion than other breeds, especially in depth across the jowls (except perhaps in its descendant, the American Quarter Horse) with a triangular shape diminishing rapidly to a small and fine muzzle, giving more nearly the appearance of the gazelle or deer. The muzzle is small and may be enwrapped in the palm of the hand. The lips are thin and fine and nostrils long, thin, and delicately curled, running upward and projecting outward. When the Arab is excited or in action, the nostrils are capable of great dilation and, seen in profile, project beyond the muzzle, giving a bold, square, sharp, and vigorous expression.

The face is slightly dished below the eyes, the cheek bones sharply cut. The eyes, set far apart, somewhat on the side of the head, are large, lustrous, kind, and full of fire when aroused. Added brain capacity is frequently present in slight protrusions over the forehead extending to just below the eyes. These protrusions are greatly prized by Arabian owners and are called *Jibbahs*. A ratio of two or two and a half to one between the circumference of the head around the jowls and the circumference directly above the nostrils is not uncommon. The cheek bones spread wide apart at the throat, often between five and six inches, enabling the muzzle to be drawn in without compressing the windpipe; hence breathing is accomplished without distress when running at speed. The ears are smaller and more sharply pointed in the males than the females. In both, the ears are set evenly together in an upright position and have great flexibility. Thus the Arab head may be visualized as lean and full of fine lines (drawings), showing intelligence, energy, courage, combined with nobility and sagacity.

The neck is long, arched, and light and sets into high, well-back withers. The throat is large and well developed, loose and pliant when at rest, and well detached from the rest of the head. The head is set on the neck at a slightly more oblique angle than in other breeds. The direct way in which the neck leaves the head for a slight distance before curving is greatly prized by Arabian owners and is called *Mitbah*.

The forequarters are high at the joining of the withers, set well back, and are heavily muscled on both sides. Shoulders are long, deep, broad at the base, and powerful, but light at the points. The arms are oblique and muscular, the forearm broad at the elbow, long and muscular; knees large, square, and deep. The cannon bone is short, flat, and clean, of good size and with exceptionally strong heavy tendons. The fetlock joint is exceptionally large and bold, the pasterns long, sloping, very elastic, and strong. Legs are set parallel in front, straight from the side, and toe facing squarely ahead.

The middle, from the front to the rear, shows the ribs *bowing out* (as in bow and arrow), and protruding beyond the quarters, somewhat like a well-formed barrel. The ribs run to a great depth beneath the chest and have ample heart and lung capacity. The ribs hold their size and are close-coupled to the point of the hip bone. The back is unusually short, with one less lumbar vertebra (as previously explained).

The hind quarters: the croup of the Arab is even with the withers of the forequarters (of the same level), the loins broad, the haunch long in proportion, quite horizontal, well rounded; the tail bone has fewer vertebrae than other breeds, as previously explained. The quarters are long, well muscled, and somewhat narrow with a fine line denoting speed. The hams are well filled out, the hocks clean, well *let down,* of almost abnormal size and strength, giving great leverage to the tendons at the gaskins. The shank bone is flat, clean, and short, with large tendons, the pasterns sloping and muscular. The fetlock joint is of exceptional size. The hind legs are vertically placed squarely under the hind quarters and parallel to the body.

The hoofs of Arabs are medium-sized and rounded, wide, hard (flinty), and low at the heels.

OTHER CHARACTERISTICS: The natural gaits are the gallop and fast flat-footed walk. In the latter, the hind feet often overstep the fore feet from twelve to thirty-six inches. While not a natural gait, the trot may be developed quickly because of the Arab's dexterity, ability, and capacity to respond to training for any equine activity or pursuit.

By reason of the desert origin of the Arab breed and its use on long treks in commerce and at war, they became accustomed to subsist on small quantities of forage and grain, also to forego water for several hours or even for days. Consequently, the stomach is smaller than that of most breeds and the amount of feed and water to sustain them and keep them in good health, vigorous, and in prime condition is generally much less than for other horses of comparable size.

Arabians are affectionate, gentle, born without fear of man or beast, and are renowned for their beauty, courage, docility, endurance, gentleness, intelligence, ruggedness, tractability, and the like and also for their romantic place in history.

Many truly great of the Arab breed, both male and female, have successfully competed in every equine contest known to man. However, a listing of the great and "the immortals" will not be attempted here for several reasons, two of which are the tremendous number it would entail, and the writer's deficiency in knowledge of the breed; a vast amount of time would be required in research to justify a listing. Yet two immortals must be mentioned, the greatest of all the great equine progenitors, the Darley Arabian and the Godolphin Arabian.

In assembling data on the origin, characteristics, and principal uses of the light horse and miniature breeds, the Arab breed filled me with a profound appreciation of its contribution to the qualities of many of the primary breeds extant.

Principal Uses

Showing under saddle, in hand, and in harness in Arabian classes and also in competition with other breeds. Showing in stock classes (Western type) in competition with other breeds. Flat and hurdle racing from one and a half miles upward to three miles.

Used as parade mounts, endurance trial horses, jumpers, and some as polo mounts; also used for hunting, and many are used for general work and pleasure riding: the latter in both English saddles and Western tack, by both sexes and all ages.

Registry

The Arabian Horse Club Registry of America, 120 South LaSalle Street, Chicago, Illinois.

Ata Aia, Mare   Dam: Mirzaia
   Sire: Katar   By: Imp. Mirzam

Owner: Jordan Arabian Farm, Mr. and Mrs. Edward B. Jordan, Fairport, New York.

Indraff, Stallion   Dam: Imp. Indaia
   Sire: Imp. Raffles   By: Raseem

Owner: Al-Marah Arabian Farm, Mr. and Mrs. Garvin E. Tankersley, Washington,
   D.C.

Alyfar, Stallion   Dam: Farnasa
Sire: Alyf   By: Nasik

Owner: Beacon Hill Farm, Mr. and Mrs. Arthur Godfrey, Paeonian Springs, Virginia.

Stardai, Mare   Dam: Zardai
Sire: Starrabi   By: Ibn Nusi

Jordan Arabian Farm, Mr. and Mrs. Edward B. Jordan, Fairport, New York.

Stardana, Filly (1)   Dam: Adana
   Sire: Starrabi   By: Ghass

Jordan Arabian Farm, Mr. and Mrs. Edward B. Jordan, Fairport, New York.

Broodmares and Foals
   Owner: Joder Arabian Farm, Anna Best Joder, Boulder, Colorado.

Jordan, Stallion
    Sire: Rafik

Dam: Mina
    By: Ahamed

Stardai, Mare
    Sire: Starrabi

Rider: Mrs. Edward B. Jordan

Owner: Jordan Arabian Farm, Mr. and Mrs. Edward B. Jordan, Fairport, New York.

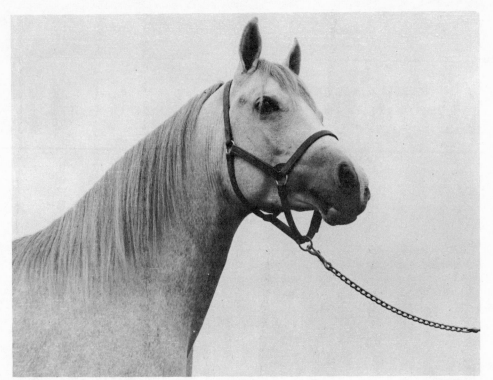

Al-Marah Radames, Stallion
Sire: Indraff

Dam: Gutne
By: Bazled

Al-Marah Rooz, Stallion
Sire: Indraff

Dam: Rose of Luzon
By: Gulastra

Handler: Mrs. Garvin E. Tankersley

Owner: Al-Marah Arabian Farm, Mr. and Mrs. Garvin E. Tankersley, Washington, D.C.

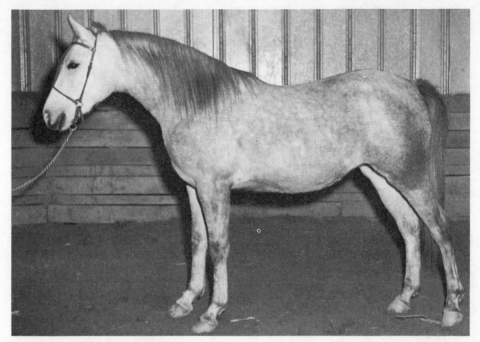

Al-Marah Rose Anne, Filly (2)   Dam: Rose Marie
    Sire: Indraff   By: Imp. Raffles

Owner: Al-Marah Arabian Farm, Mr. and Mrs. Garvin E. Tankersley, Washington, D.C.

Broodmares and Foals
    Jordan Arabian Farm, Mr. and Mrs. Edward B. Jordan, Fairport, New York.

Broodmares and Foals
    Owner: Joder Arabian Farm, Anna Best Joder, Boulder, Colorado.

Stardai, Mare   Handler: Mrs. Edward B. Jordan
  Sire: Starrabi
    Owner: Jordan Arabian Farm, Mr. and Mrs. Edward B. Jordan, Fairport, New York.

Rakiz, Horse
Rider: John Barringer

Owner: Snake River Arabian Stud,
Dr. and Mrs. Ward A. Rulien,
Glenns Ferry, Idaho.

Casanova, Horse
Sire: Ronek

Rider: Miss Beverly Vehrs
Owner: Mr. J. E. McElroy, Richland, Washington.

Zab, Horse
   Sire: Fay El Dine

Rider: Joseph Toth

Owner: Mr. G. L. Wirtz, Sr., Kutztown, Pennsylvania.

Al-Marah El Hezzez, Horse
   Sire: Indraff

Rider: Harold Brite

Owner: Dr. R. L. MacTavish, Hudson Heights, New Jersey.

Al-Marah Radames, Horse
   Sire: Indraff

Rider: Mrs. Garvin E. Tankersley

Owner: Al-Marah Arabian Farm, Mr. and Mrs. Garvin E. Tankersley, Washington, D.C.

Rasan, Horse   Driver: Miss Carolyn Davis

Owner: Dr. and Mrs. R. E. LaRue, Erie, Illinois.

Bint Rihani, Mare   Rider: Miss Barbara Tignar

Owner: Joder Arabian Farm, Anna Best Joder, Boulder, Colorado.

Ibn Rogue, Horse   Rider: Miss Helen C. Lee
Owner: Joder Arabian Farm, Anna Best Joder, Boulder, Colorado.

Roseana, Mare   Rider: Miss Mona Betts
Owner: Circle 2 Arabians, Mr. and Mrs. Burr Betts, Englewood, Colorado.

Rose Marie, Mare
    Sire: Imp. Raffles

Dam: Rodetta
By: Agwe

Al-Marah Rose Susan, Foal
    Sire: Indraff

  Owner: Al-Marah Arabian Farm, Mr. and Mrs. Garvin E. Tankersley, Washington,
    D.C.

Broodmares

Owner: Jordan Arabian Farm, Mr. and Mrs. Edward B. Jordan, Fairport, New York.

Whitewood Cornpone, Gelding
Sire: Laralley Pride

Rider: Miss Carol Johnson

Owner: Laxfield Farm, Weston, Massachusetts.

Connemara

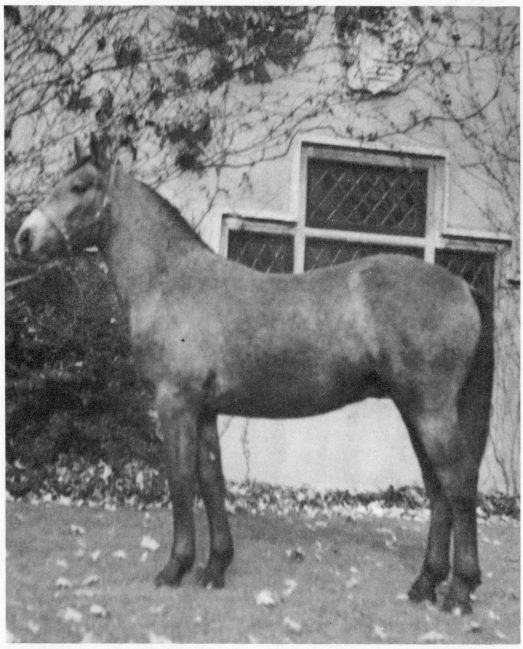

Imp. Lystra Lad, Colt (1) Dam: Screeba Roan
Sire: Creg Coneera By: Calla Rebel
Owner: Lystra Farm, Mr. Harry S. Middendorf, Hamilton, Massachusetts.

Connemara

Origin

PLACE OF ORIGIN: Ireland, West Coast.

FOUNDATION: The original foundation stock of the Connemara is obscure in history. However, there are many interesting and established facts about the breed's origin.

It is established that hardy small horses, believed to be of Icelandic origin, existed on the west coast of Ireland for many generations, under most difficult conditions among the bogs and the rocky hills. They subsisted by grazing on the gorse and heather. In this rugged environment and with limited feeding they became smaller but acquired surefootedness by avoiding quagmires and other pitfalls and by cantering up and down the hilly, rocky terrain. Such was their lot and it resulted in their becoming the foundation of one of the hardiest, most self-reliant breeds extant.

In later years, when crossed first with Andalusian horses and Spanish Barb horses that escaped from the wreck of the Spanish Armada off the coast of Ireland, later with the stallions of those breeds imported by Galway merchants and, still later, crossed with imported stallions of the Arab breed, the breed known as the Connemara Pony came into being, and is now officially registered through the founding of a Registry (Stud Book): *The Connemara Pony Stud Book*, presently of Galway, Eire.

The Arab characteristics are evident in the modern-day Connemara: the expressive eyes, the carriage, the soundness. Occasionally the slightly dished face of the Arab is evident in the Connemara. In recent years there have been many importations to the United States and the formation of an American Connemara Pony Society became expedient for the registration of importations and of those bred in this country. In December 1956, the American Connemara Pony Society was formed under the auspices of the Connemara Pony

Society of Galway, Eire, and of the English Connemara Pony Society.

The primary foundation sire of the Connemara was Rebel, whose name appears in practically every modern-day pedigree tabulation. Another was Cannon Ball, whose prepotency is evident in many pedigrees.

A listing of the great performers of full Connemara blood, or with its admixture, is an impossibility; however, below are a few:

Cannon Ball and Rebel, both great progenitors of the breed, mentioned above.

Karbous, sired by an Arab-Barb whose dam was a Connemara. A brilliant jumper and winner of the Irish Three Day Event.

Little Squire, a Connemara. A champion jumper, in high society for many years, openly competing with horses.

The Nugget, a Connemara. A champion jumper, in high society for some twenty years.

Pretty Polly, an Arab-Connemara. Famous as the ideal type of riding pony.

Characteristics

COLOR: Bay, black, brown, cream dun, and gray and, occasionally, chestnut and roan. Piebald and skewbald colorings are excluded from registration.

SIZE: Height varies from thirteen (13.0) hands to fourteen two (14.2) hands. Weight varies from 700 pounds to 850 pounds.

OTHER CHARACTERISTICS: Exceptionally docile, intelligent, and tractable, and ideal as children's mounts. They are extremely hardy, with unusual weight-carrying and staying power, require a minimum amount of grain, forage, and attention in order to maintain good flesh and health: easy keepers. The breed is also noted for its compact body, strong, slightly sloping shoulder, clean, flat, hard leg bones, good feet, and soundness.

Principal Uses

Showing under saddle and occasionally in harness, and for general riding and hunting by medium-sized adults and children. They are particularly noted, in fact are famous, as open jumpers.

Registration

PURE BRED DIVISION: All ponies registered in the *Connemara Stud Book*, Galway, Eire. All ponies two years or over may be permanently registered and all ponies under two years may be issued a temporary registration, etc., in accordance with the rules and regulations of the Society.

HALF-BRED DIVISION: All ponies sired by a registered Connemara Pony stallion are eligible for registration in a *Supplement* to the *Pure Bred Stud Book*. In the third generation, the progeny of a half-bred Connemara stallion or mare is eligible for entry in the *Pure Bred Stud Book*, providing all intervening crosses have been to registered Connemara Ponies, etc.

Registry

American Connemara Pony Society, Round Robin Farm, East Pepperell, Massachusetts.

Whitewood Biscuit, Mare   Rider: Miss Jeannie Eaton
  Sire: Laralley Pride

Owner: Mrs. William C. Crane, Jr., Whitewood Stud, The Plains, Virginia.

Imp. Wicklow Mountain Rose Bay, Mare   Rider: Mrs. Bruce Read
    Sire: Mac Dara

Owner: Round Robin Farm, Mrs. Bruce Read, East Pepperell, Massachusetts.

Squire, Gelding   Little Squire, Gelding
   Rider: Danny Shea   Rider: Johnny Meeney
      Owner: Mr. Danny Shea, Merryland Farm, Hyde, Maryland.

Cassilis Minuet, Filly (3)
Sire: Cassilis Masterpiece

Owner: Hillingdon Farm, Mr. Graham C. Woodruff, New Marlboro, Massachusetts.

Hackney

Minaret of Hillingdon, Filly (2)
Sire: Whippoorwill Lillymaster

Owner: Hillingdon Farm, Mr. Graham C. Woodruff, New Marlboro, Massachusetts.

Hackney

Origin

PLACE OF ORIGIN: England. American Hackney: throughout the United States and Canada.

FOUNDATION: History makes evident that England had a breed of trotting horses during the Middle Ages and the Tudor era. Norfolk Trotters were valuable and costly animals in those days, as in 1470 it was indicated that the price of one of Barney's Horses was twenty marks (a mark was worth about 13s. 4d.) and "not one penny less would be taken." Considerable legislation was directed toward improving the breed of horses, especially Road Horses, as 33d Henry VIII, C.5, A.D. 1542; the last clause thereof plainly distinguishes trotting horses from cart horses and sumpter horses (pack animals).

In the March 29, 1755 issue of the *Cambridge Journal,* an advertisement sets forth the breeding of Sampson (Robinson's), foaled in 1745; he is a son of Blaze. Mambrino, a trotter-racer, the progenitor of many American Standardbreds and American Thoroughbreds, also traces back to Blaze.

Messrs. John Lawrence and John Marshall were well qualified to write on equine breeding and equine activities, both contemporaneous and historic. History records that Sampson was sired by Blaze (not a son) out of a Hunter mare. It was also pretended that he was out of a daughter of the Thoroughbred Hartley's Hip. This was challenged by John Lawrence in his *Treatise on Horses,* 3d Edition, Vol. 1, pp. 222-223: *"The Hostler who led Sampson's dam to Blaze* and who afterwards bitted [bridled] and broke [trained and educated] the foal [Sampson], repeatedly asserted that the pedigree of the mare [his dam] was unknown, but she appeared to be about three parts bred [a three-quarter thoroughbred]."

The reader should understand that in the early days of the horse (any breed), breeding records were privately maintained if at all, and their accuracy largely depended on the honesty and integrity of the owners of the animals. When associations, clubs, or societies were formed and they established registers (stud books) there was bound to be a hodgepodge of data to analyze and, for the most part, each such registry came up with a commendable record of the horses registered. True, many revisions occurred and many errors remain. Selective breeding (breeding the best stallions to the best mares) and the lapse of time have practically and technically eliminated the identification and classification errors of both omission and commission.

In the Yorkshire districts of England the running racer was strongly entrenched with prejudice toward the trotter racer. Early advertisements in the daily and weekly press in those districts (the counties of Cambridge, Lincoln, Norfolk, and Suffolk), mention Frank Maw's Sportman by Sportsman out of Lord Clermont's Wentworth, a son of the Saanah Arabian, as *allowed to be the first trotter in Yorkshire*. It is subject to two interpretations: (1) Allowed (permitted) to stand for service (at stud) in Yorkshire; (2) Allowed (believed) to be the best trotting stallion of trotting proclivity in Yorkshire. The author interprets it to be the latter, although prejudice did and does exist between dyed-in-the-wool Thoroughbred enthusiasts and Trotting enthusiasts.

Another trotting stallion that attained fame in the Yorkshire districts was Quaker of Kendal by Westmoreland dam by Ironsides. It is said of him that he trotted eight miles in 25 minutes and 36 seconds, carrying 238 pounds, and sixteen miles within the hour, carrying 224 pounds. The reader should understand that trotting was largely under saddle in the early days in England and the United States and to a great extent is so nowadays in France; often trotting was mixed, that is, both under saddle and in harness in the same race and frequently still is in France.

John Marshall is due a tribute for doing so much to publicize the trotting horses (road horses) of the Yorkshire districts. He particularly mentions that Jalap, a Thoroughbred stallion, by Regulus, a son of the Godolphin Arabian out of a granddaughter of Flying Childers, sired excellent stock out of the native road mares and made his name famous with the farmers of the district. One son of Jalap, known as Trotting Jalap, was the progenitor of many animals whose trotting actions were excellent.

In John Lawrence's *Treatise on Horses*, mention is made of the system of breeding in Norfolk, which resulted in producing a number of Hackney horses before the year 1796. The Norfolk *Chronicle* and the Norfolk *Mercury*, newspapers circulating in all parts of Norfolk and Cambridgeshire from the years 1750 to 1830, were favored media in announcing the rounds of Thoroughbred stallions and Trotting stallions. "Rounds" means the list of places at which the stallion is to be stationed on certain dates for the purpose of serving local mares.

In advertisements in the local press during the years 1772 and 1773, the announcement of the availability of a stallion's service reads, in part, as follows: "The noted Scots' or Shales' Horse [also sometimes referred to as the Shields' Horse] will cover the season at Long Sutton, in Lincolnshire, at one guinea a mare and one shilling to the servant [the stallioneer], the money to be paid at the stable door, no returns." "No Returns" means that each service would *stand* as completed whether conception occurred or not. "He was got [sired] by a son of Blaze and he [Blaze] was by Flying Childers [by Darley Arabian] out of a Hackney mare."

From the columns of the Norfolk *Chronicle* and the Norwich *Mercury*, it may be gleaned that the horse (stallion) variously known as Scots' or Shales' or Shields' Horse was the first noteworthy Hackney stallion of the modern type, but John Lawrence states, in his *History of the Horse*, that "His sire was The Duke of Lancaster's Blank by the Godolphin Arabian out of the Little Hartley Mare which was got [sired] by Bartley's Childers out of the Large Hartley Mare, a mare rich in Arab blood and Barb blood."

The Norfolk Trotter Bellfounder, foaled in 1816, is registered in the English *Hackney Stud Book* as Bellfounder—Jarys', No. 55, and his influence on the American Standardbred is of profound sig-

nificance as the sire of the Charles Kent mare, dam of Hambletonian 10 (Rysdyk's Hambletonian), foundation sire of the Standardbred breed. As Bellfounder was the first Registered Hackney
imported to the United States his pedigree, as recorded (registered)
in *The American Hackney Stud Book,* is set forth:

Pedigree of

Bellfounder—Jarys' 55

Foaled 1816. Bay. Fifteen (15.0) Hands. Owner and Breeder:
Roger Jary, Ashell and Harding—Norfolk, England.

Sires

   I Bellfounder (Stevens') 52 dam by Smuggler, 789.
  II Pretender (Wroots') 596 dam by Joseph Andrews.
 III Fire Away 201, dam Jenkinson's Mare by Joseph Andrews.
 IV Driver 187, dam of Foxhunter son of Sampson.
  V Original Shales 690, the horse regarded as the earliest to which
      Norfolk Hackneys are traceable satisfactorily. His dam is re-
      corded as a Hackney mare and the year of his birth 1755.
 VI Blaze (1733-1756), dam Confederate Filly by Grey Grantham,
      son of the Brown Lord Turk.
VII Flying Childers by the Darley Arabian and out of the mare
      Betty Leeds, a daughter of Careless by Spanker, a son of
      D'Arcy Yellow Turk.

Dams

   I Velocity (Mr. Roger Jarys'), said to be by Haphazard, a son
     of Sir Peter out of Miss Hervey by Eclipse.

II Described as a Yorkshire Mare.

The reader will note that:

1. Bellfounder is traced to seven sires and only two dams and those incompletely. This is prevalent in the older pedigree tabulations and is the result of the importance (then believed) of the tail-male ancestry or lineage over the tail-female ancestry and the lack of information on mares.

2. Original Shales 690 is shown as being sired by Blaze, whereas hereinbefore Mr. John Lawrence states in his *History of the Horse* (not exactly quoted here): The sire of Scots' or Shales' or Shields' Horse (the Original Shales 690, in the above pedigree Tabulation) was The Duke of Lancaster's Blank.

3. As both Blaze and Blank had a strong admixture of Arab blood and Barb blood the writer feels, to use the vernacular, that it makes no never mind which sired Original Shales 690.

4. It is easy to understand that the pedigrees of early horses might have many errors of omission and of commission. The best proof of true blood is that it must be consistent in reproduction performance and in task performance. (Task performance means performance on the rack track, in the show ring, in endurance trials, in cattle handling, and the like.) Insofar as the writer has knowledge, neither Blaze nor Blank has been successfully challenged as failing in any way as a progenitor.

Characteristics

COLOR: Bay, brown, black, chestnut, roan, and sorrel.

SIZE: Horses: Height varies from fourteen two (14.2) hands to sixteen (16.0) hands, sometimes over. Weight varies from 900 pounds to 1,200 pounds.

Ponies (Bantams): Height varies from 44 inches or eleven (11.0) hands to not over 58 inches or fourteen two (14.2) hands. Weight varies from 650 pounds to 850 pounds.

Small Hackneys (referred to as Hackney Ponies and sometimes as Bantam Hackneys) were established many years ago by crossing small-sized Hackneys with Welsh Ponies, with small-sized Arabs and Thoroughbreds, and also small Hackneys to small Hackneys. As their size and characteristics became fixed, they have usually in the last fifty years been crossed, small Hackney to small Hackney, with resultant miniature sizes and well-defined pony characteristics.

The *Registry* (*Stud Book*) of the American Hackney Horse Society does not distinguish between *horse* and *pony*. In other words, the produce or offspring of a full-sized Hackney stallion and a small-sized Hackney mare, or vice versa, is eligible for registration, regardless of size or without definement.

As small Hackneys have well-defined pony characteristics and the Society (as well as others) refers to them as Hackney Ponies, the writer desires to take exception thereto, on technical grounds (hopefully without prejudice). It is his opinion that *horse* and *pony* should be defined in its rules of registration and thus segregated before small Hackneys may be properly designated Hackney Ponies.

In many countries of the world, small-sized horses exist and they are invariably designated *as horses*. It is true, of course, that such small-sized horses do not have miniature or pony characteristics, as witness the small Icelandic horses; it is incorrect to refer to them *as ponies*.

OTHER CHARACTERISTICS (AND LORE): The distinctive name Hackney (formerly Hackneye) evolved from *nag, hack horse,* and the Anglo-Saxon *hnaegan,* to neigh. The Normans introduced their own familiar appellation thus: Hakenay or Hacknay (*haquenée*), a French word with ultimate derivation unknown but possibly from the Latin *equus,* horse. The word trotter (*trotta*), descriptive of the characteristics of the gait of such a horse, evolved at least as early as 1465.

In a report of sales at Saint Faith's Fair, three trotters were sold—right fair horses. The word Roadster is synonymous with the word Hackney.

In the 1803 issue of the *Sporting Dictionary and Rural Depository*, the following appears, in part:

Hackney is the general acceptation of the word, within the sporting world, of a horse superior to all others upon the score of utility; being rendered subservient to every office or exertion, speed, or perseverance, or in other words, to all the drudgery and labor of his situation, from which his contemporaries, the racer, the hunter, and the charger, by the imaginary superiority of their qualifications and pampered appearance, are always exempt. . . . It is the peculiar province of the Hackney to carry his master 12 or 15 miles in an hour to covert, where the hunter (guide) is in waiting, and after the hunt is over to be ridden back by the groom with great expedition, in order to do his many chores. . . . It is in the department of the Hackney to encounter and overcome emergencies and difficulties of every description; his constitution should be excellent and his spirit invincible; he must be enabled to go five and twenty miles or thirty miles at a stage *without drawing bit* and without the least respect to the depth of the roads, or the dreary state of the weather; and if he not be equal to any weight, in these trying exertions, he will be held in no estimation as a Hackney of Fashion.

Hackneys are docile, intelligent, and tractable. They are hardy, spirited (but gentle), with unusual energy and endurance. They subsist in good flesh and health, generally, on a minimum amount of grains and forage. They are noted for high, forceful, four-square, knee and hock, "poetry of motion" action.

Principal Uses

Showing in heavy harness, single, double team (pair), tandem team (pair), and four-in-hand. Showing under saddle, high jumping, pleasure riding, and some harness racing.

Registry

The American Hackney Horse Society, 26-05 Fair Lawn Avenue, Fair Lawn, New Jersey.

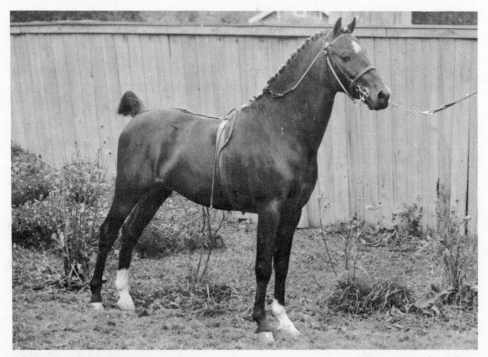

Whippoorwill Masterpiece, Stallion   Dam: Cassilis Lily
Sire: Cassilis Masterpiece   By: Mighty Swell

Owner: Whippoorwill Farm, Mr. and Mrs. J. Dean Bigford, New Marlboro, Massachusetts.

Cassilis Glen Ideal, Horse
Sire: Cassilis Masterpiece

Driver: J. Dean Bigford

Cassilis Sir Echo, Colt (3)
Sire: Echo of Hillingdon

Driver: Mrs. J. Macy Willets

Owner: Hillingdon Farm, Mr. Graham C. Woodruff, New Marlboro, Massachusetts.

Dream of Hillingdon, Mare   Driver: Mr. Graham C. Woodruff
 Sire: Cassilis Masterpiece

Minaret of Hillingdon, Mare   Driver: Mrs. J. Macy Willets
 Sire: Whippoorwill Lillymaster

Owner: Hillingdon Farm, Mr. Graham C. Woodruff, New Marlboro, Massachusetts.

Cora's Mite, Mare   Driver: Mrs. F. L. Van Lennep
   Sire: King's Banner

Karen, Mare   Driver: Mrs. Reed Bridgford
   Sire: King's Banner

Owner: Dodge Stables, Mr. and Mrs. F. L. Van Lennep, Rochester, Michigan.

Red Letter, Horse
Sire: King's Banner

Dam: Victory Song
By: Coronation

Driver: Reed Bridgford

Owner: Dodge Stables, Mr. and Mrs. F. L. Van Lennep, Rochester, Michigan.

Dream of Hillingdon, Mare
Sire: Cassilis Masterpiece

Echo of Hillingdon, Horse
Sire: Cassilis Masterpiece

Driver: J. Dean Bigford

Owner: Hillingdon Farm, Mr. Graham C. Woodruff, New Marlboro, Massachusetts.

Windcrest Donfield, Stallion
Sire: Upwey Ben Don

Dam: Seneca Sweetheart
By: Cornwallis

Owners: Waseeka Farm, Mrs. D. D. Power and Mr. and Mrs. E. K. Annis, Ashland, Massachusetts.

Morgan

Lippitt Mandate, Horse   Rider: Master Robert Mathias

Owner: Mrs. Harold L. Childs, Ringtown, Pennsylvania.

Morgan

Origin

PLACE OF ORIGIN: United States, within the New England states; especially Vermont.

FOUNDATION: The foundation stallion was Justin Morgan, one of two stallions that established recognized American breeds singlehandedly. The other such stallion was Old King, which established the American Albino breed, greatly aided by mares of the Morgan breed. Justin Morgan was foaled around 1790 in West Springfield, Massachusetts and was taken to Vermont at between two and three years of age. He led a strenuous and active long life and died in 1821 at approximately thirty-two years of age.

Little is known (proved) about Justin Morgan's breeding. It is stated that "His sire is True Briton or Beautiful Bay of Thoroughbred lineage, descending from Arabians" and "His dam is of Wildair Breeding, and admixture of Arab, Barb, and Turk Blood."

The stated siring of Justin Morgan is subject to these conclusions:

1. His dam was bred to two stallions; first, to the cover of True Briton and second, to the cover of Beautiful Bay.
2. His dam was covered by either True Briton or Beautiful Bay.
3. True Briton and Beautiful Bay are different names of the same stallion.

In those days as well as nowadays, within certain breeds in which public activity or competition is not restricted to identification by registration (Certificates of Registration), names were (and now are) frequently changed by new owners and by fancy or whim, within the same ownership. In the absence of confirmation of the name of the sire of Justin Morgan, the writer favors the conclusion that True Briton and Beautiful Bay are different names by which his sire was known.

105

The breeding of Justin Morgan's dam is shown in Volume I of *The Morgan Horse and Register* as "The Wildair mare sired by Diamond by Church's Wildair of the same blood as True Briton" and "Diamond's dam and the second dam of Justin Morgan were of unknown breeding."

It is known that mares in the New England states at the time of the conception of Justin Morgan were of varied breeding: the Norfolk Trotter (England), the Dutch Horse (Holland), and the Norwegian Dun (Norway). Both the Dutch Horse and the Norwegian Dun are small, thick-set, and sturdy. The Norwegian Duns are exceptionally blocky and compact with small sharp ears, deep barrel, fairly level croup, full square quarters, with sturdy short but trim legs and concave flintlike feet. In addition, they are dun in color as well as in name and have medium manes and tails and medium hair on their legs and fetlocks, whereas the Dutch Horses are *light draft horses, short-legged, heavy-bodied, with thick long manes and tails and with hairy legs and fetlocks*. The Norwegian Dun's influence on the mares brought to America via England, during early Colonial days, was of considerable significance.

The writer is aware of the documentation that Justin Morgan was reasonably believed to stem from a dam of predominantly Dutch Horse with an admixture of Arab and that the physical structure of the Morgan breed, starting with the family founder Justin Morgan, is attributable to the phenomenon of mutation. Mutation is a change, an alteration in form or quality, a sudden variation, the offspring differing from its parents in some well-marked characteristic, owing to changes within chromosomes or genes. A mutant is one that undergoes mutation, a genetic variation that breeds true. The writer is of the considered opinion that Justin Morgan's dam was highly endowed with Norwegian Dun blood and from it evolved Justin Morgan's "four-square blocky stature" and other quality characteristics. The fact that the dun coloring of the Norwegian Duns has not shown up to an appreciable degree, if at all, is understandable because of the strength of coloring in the "Horses of the East," Arab, Barb, and Turk, in the sire of Justin Morgan and perhaps to a degree in his dam. Whatever the combination of blood coursing his veins, whatever the genes from which he evolved, it was prepotent to the nth degree and continues in his descendants, generation after generation.

Justin Morgan was around fourteen (14.0) hands high and weighed around 950 pounds. He was a bay (almost brown) with black points: legs, mane, and tail. He was used for general work, for riding, and frequently competed in trotting races and running races at limited distances. During the years he sired numerous foals that aided in the upgrading of the general utility horse. His blood has been perpetuated through many sons but principally through the three sons, Sherman, Bulrush, and Woodbury. He also aided materially in the establishment of other American breeds, especially the American Albino, American Saddlebred, Standardbred, and Tennessee Walking Horse. The maternal side of the world's champion pacing stallion, the immortal Dan Patch, 1:55 1/4, is strongly infused with Morgan blood.

Characteristics

COLOR: Bay, black (uncommon), brown, and chestnut. Extensive white markings are uncommon.

SIZE: Height varies from fourteen (14.0) hands to fifteen two (15.2) hands. Weight varies from 900 pounds to 1,200 pounds.

OTHER CHARACTERISTICS: The Morgans of today are generally larger and finer than their foundation sire, Justin Morgan, from years of selective breeding and feeding.

Their style, trimness, easy-keeping qualities, courage, docility, energy, endurance, spirit, sturdiness, and above all intelligence and versatility are ever present.

Principal Uses

Under saddle: showing, racing at the trot, jumping, and stock handling.

In harness: showing, single and double, and racing at the trot; also pulling contests.

Also used for general utility and farm work and as a pleasure horse in harness and under saddle.

Registry

The Morgan Horse Club, Inc., 90 Broad Street, New York, New York.

Broodmare

Owner: Richards Ranch, Mrs. W. T. Richards, Pine City, New York.

Broodmare and Foal

Owner: Richards Ranch, Mr. and Mrs. W. J. Richards, Pine City, New York.

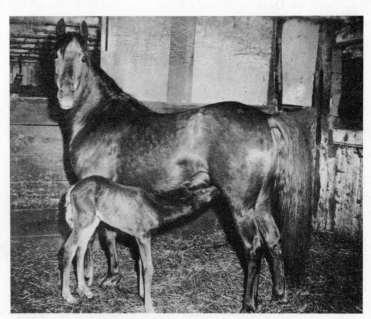

Red, Horse   Dam: An Arab   Broodmare and Foal
Sire: A Morgan

Rider: Mrs. W. J. Richards

Owner: Richards Ranch, Mr. and Mrs. W. J. Richards, Pine City, New York.

Windcrest Sentimental Lady, Mare   Rider: Mrs. E. K. Annis
    Sire: Upwey Ben Don

  Owners: Waseeka Farm, Mrs. D. D. Power and Mr. and Mrs. E. K. Annis, Ashland,
   Massachusetts.

Windcrest Donfield, Horse   Driver: John Lydon

  Owners: Mrs. D. D. Power and Mr. and Mrs. E. K. Annis, Ashland, Massachusetts.

Lippitt Mandate, Horse   Driver: Mr. Harold L. Childs

Lippitt Mandate, Horse   Driver: Mrs. Harold L. Childs

Owner: Mrs. Harold L. Childs, Ringtown, Pennsylvania.

Nancy Ann, Mare
  Sire: Lippitt Moro Ash

Rider: Mrs. W. T. Richards

Little Miss Pepper, Mare
  Sire: Brown Pepper

Rider: Mrs. W. T. Richards

Owner: Richards Ranch,

Mrs. W. T. Richards,

Pine City, New York.

Top Hat, Stallion (Quarter Horse)   Dam: Noelke Mare
Sire: Buck   By: Clegg Sorrel

Owner: The Glory Ranch, Dolson and Mary Gilbert, Calabasas, California.

Palomino

Golden Belle, Mare   Rider: Miss Eileen Bastek
Sire: Androcles

Owner: Mr. Sam Forgotson, Milltown, New Jersey.

Palomino

Origin

PLACE OF ORIGIN: United States; all Western states for the heavier parade and Western types, and California, the Southern, and Middle Eastern states for the lighter-gaited, harness, parade, and jumping types.

FOUNDATION: Palominos are of ancient origin. Proof of it is evident in art collections; Rembrandt's "The Rape of Europa," painted in 1632, depicts four Palomino horses; the painting "Hunting in Lo Tai" (the artist unknown to the writer) depicts an emperor of China astride a golden Palomino. History relates other instances of Palominos before the sixteenth century. Cortez brought Palominos from Spain to Mexico in 1519 and they were used during the invasion. The endurance of Palomino horses was demonstrated in 1800 when General John C. Fremont, desiring to make a quick trip from Los Angeles to Monterey and return (a round trip distance of some 800 miles), borrowed Palominos from Sr. Don Estaban, Mayor de Gano (Foreman of the Cattle) of Santa Barbara Mission. William Heath Davis, an early settler of California, described the beautiful Palominos used in a wedding cavalcade in 1838.

Foundation stallions primarily responsible for infusing characteristics and coloring, particularly in the Western type of Palominos, are Plaudit and Sappho. Others have materially contributed, so many in fact that, inasmuch as this is not a treatise on the Palomino breed, space does not permit a complete listing thereof. A few of those, alphabetically arranged, are: 1. Booger Bear; 2. Del Monte; 3. Golden Cavalier; 4. Gold Dust; 5. Gold Heels; 6. Golden Don; 7. Out Play; 8. Play Boy; 9. Revel's Cream of Wheat; 10. Sober; 11. The Harvester; 12. Titantic.

115

Characteristics

COLOR: The Palomino is a color breed and the primary requisites are, specifically: Body like a newly minted gold coin (varying to darker and lighter shadings), with dark skin, ivory, silver, or white mane and tail, the mane and tail hairs not in excess of fifteen per cent (15%) of chestnut or dark hairs. Dark skin is not a requisite for registration by The Palomino Horse Association, Inc.

The following are not eligible for registration: blue, moon, pink, or glass eyes, and white or dark spots on the body.

SIZE: Height varies from fourteen two (14.2) hands to sixteen (16.0) hands. Weight varies from 900 pounds to 1,200 pounds. Animals under fourteen two (14.2) hands are generally not eligible for registration nor are those having the characteristics of draft horse or pony breeding or those of unknown ancestry.

OTHER CHARACTERISTICS: Exceptionally docile, friendly, and tractable. Their golden coats with white, silver, or ivory trimmings (trimmings are manes and tails) are impressive, beautiful, and brilliant whether at work, at attention, or in repose.

Principal Uses

HEAVY (LARGER) TYPE: Showing under saddle in Western tack. Parade mounts and stock handling.

LIGHT (SMALLER) TYPE: Showing under English-type saddle in both three-gaited and five-gaited classes. Also shown in harness in fine harness classes. Showing under saddle in Western tack. Also as jumpers, parade mounts, polo mounts, and stock handling.

Some are world-famous as performers: 1. Goldie (Catoctin Gold), a favorite mount of Arthur Godfrey. 2. Nautical (Peter de Oro), a favorite mount of the United States Equestrian Team. 3. Trigger (Golden Cloud), and Trigger, Jr. (Golden Zephyr), are favorite mounts of Roy Rogers.

Registries

The Palomino Horse Association, Inc., P. O. Box 446, Reseda, California.

Palomino Horse Breeders of America, P. O. Box 82, Mineral Wells, Texas.

Golden Belle, Mare
Sire: Androcles

Owner: Mr. Sam Forgotson, Milltown, New Jersey

Catoctin Gold, Horse
Sire: Gold Alla

Catoctin Gold, Horse   Rider: Mr. Arthur Godfrey
Sire: Gold Alla

Owner: Beacon Hill Farms, Mr. and Mrs. Arthur Godfrey, Paeonian Springs, Virginia.

Flying Kite, Stallion   Dam: Little Mitzie
Sire: Joe Bailey   By: Not Furnished

Owner: Mr. Ernest Esse, Karnes City, Texas.

Pinto

Trigger, Gelding
Sire: Star

    Handler: Mr. Peter J. Teller.
      Owner: Mr. Peter J. Teller, Middletown, New York.

Pinto

Origin

PLACE OF ORIGIN: United States, principally western and southwest states.

FOUNDATION: The first Pintos (*pintado,* a Spanish word, means painted, spotted, or mottled) were brought to America by Cortez and other Spanish explorers. Records indicate that among the horses brought from Spain by Cortez were two stallions of Overo type. They were believed to be of Spanish Barb stock. When Pinto stallions were turned loose to roam the plains they crossed with the native mares of the American Indian tribes and their offspring became the famous "Paints" of Western lore. South America is also a well-known area for the Pinto; a majority of them are of Overo type, whereas in North America the majority are of Tobiano type.

Until recently the Pinto was classified into four color types: Overo, Tobiano, Morocco, a variant of Tobiano, and Appaloosa. As the latter had definite breed characteristics, it was segregated from the others as a breed and established a separate *Registry (Stud Book).*

The Pinto Horse Association of America recently officially recognized two stallions for their contribution to the foundation and improvement of the modern-day American Pinto. They are: 1. Sheik, a black and white Tobiano type whose sire was Quick Return (a Registered Thoroughbred) and whose dam was La Bernita (a Pinto) by Two Step (a Pinto of American Saddlebred-Arab cross). He was a many times champion and sire of champions. 2. Sun Cloud, a bay and white Tobiano type whose sire was Beauty (a Pinto) by Sonny Boy (American Saddlebred breeding). He was a former parade horse champion and the sire of many champions, both pleasure and using horses.

The Morocco Spotted Horse is, in fact, a Tobiano-type Pinto. At one time they were exclusively registered but in recent years they have also been combined in the Pinto *Registry*. While their paternal ancestry stems from Spanish Barb stock, their maternal ancestry, unlike the other Pintos, stems from American Saddlebred, Arab, Hackney, and other breeds.

Characteristics

COLORING: The Pinto is a *color* of three types: Overo, Tobiano, and Morocco; however, the Morocco Spotted Horse is recognized as *a breed* by the National Association of Stallion Registration Boards.

The Overo's primary colors are: bay, black, brown, dun, roan, or sorrel with white as the secondary color extending in an irregular pattern; legs a combination of colors, always one colored white, if only a boot. The white extends upward from under the belly with the dorsal region (back) being colored. The head is partially or fully white. Glass or blue eyes are also a characteristic. A famous Overo-type stallion is Dor's Black Victory.

The Tobiano's primary color is white and the secondary colors are: black, brown, dun, or sorrel. The name and tail are of the coloring of the region from which they stem. The legs are white (four legs) and the head is entirely dark or marked with a blaze, star, or stripe. Some have glass eyes but they are not a common characteristic. Famous Tobiano-type horses are Baby Doll and Trigger.

The Morocco's primary color is white and the secondary colors are: black, brown, dun, or sorrel. The Morocco generally has an all-white body, with the solid color on the neck and head. In any case, the solid color must not be less than ten per cent (10%), exclusive of white legs and a star on the face (head). A famous Morocco-type stallion is Kanhwa.

SIZE: Height varies from fourteen one (14.1) hands to sixteen (16.0) hands. Weight varies from 800 pounds to 1,200 pounds. Animals under fourteen one (14.1) hands are not eligible for registration, nor are those having the characteristics of draft horse or pony breeding.

OTHER CHARACTERISTICS: Extremely docile and tractable to a degree that many children own and handle them. Whenever and wherever they appear, their attractive and showy colorings make them the cynosure of all eyes.

Principal Uses

Showing under English saddle or Western tack as parade mounts, and for riding by adults and children in general. Also for stock handling, high school dressage, gymkhana, etc.

Registration

The Pinto is registered under three distinct types:

1. Parade type of American Saddlebred, Arab, and Thoroughbred breeding.
2. Stock type of Arab, Morgan, and Quarter Horse breeding.
3. Pleasure type of all breeds.

Registry

Overo, Tobiano, and Morocco color types
  Pinto Horse Association of America, 33 Sierra Drive, Dixon, California.

Morocco Spotted Horse
  Morocco Spotted Horse Association of America, Greenfield, Iowa.

Baby Doll, Mare   *Pinto, Tobiano Type*   Dam and Sire: Not Furnished
Sire: A Pinto

Owner: Wm. and Bonnie Bailey, Kent, Ohio.

Kanhwa, Stallion   *Pinto, Morocco Type*   Dam: Madame Flash
Sire: Rex Hallmark   By: Not Furnished

Owner: Mr. Earl Speece, Jr., Marion, Ohio.

Dor's Black Victory, Stallion   *Pinto, Overo Type*   Dam and Sire: Not Furnished
Sire: An Arabian

Owner: Victory Farms, Miss Doris Hendryx, Kent, Ohio.

Lady Rose, Mare   Rider: Mrs. A. L. Albright

Silver Dawn, Mare   Rider: Dr. A. L. Albright

Owner: Dr. and Mrs. A. L. Albright, Cayuga, Indiana.

Flicka, Mare   Dam: Bettsy Ress

Sire: Star   By: Not Furnished

Owner: Mr. Peter J. Teller, Middletown, New York.

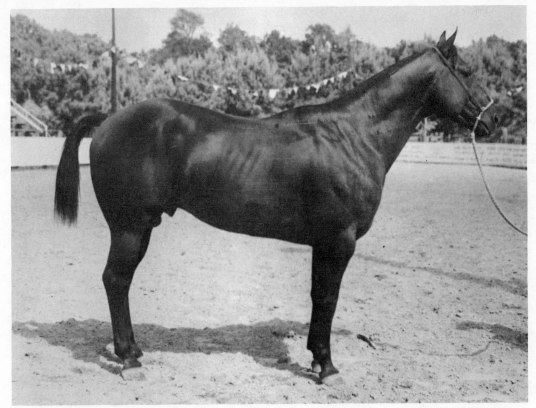

King's Joe Boy
Sire: King

Dam: Miss Alice
By: Not Furnished

Owner: Mr. John Meheens, Dermott, Arkansas.

Quarter Horse

Wig, Mare and Foal
Sire: Harmon Baker

Dam and Sire: Not Furnished

Owner: Mrs. F. B. Phillips, Jr., Dallas, Texas.

Quarter Horse

Origin

PLACE OF ORIGIN: Virginia, Carolina, and Florida in the Colonial era; in the centuries since, Texas and other southwestern states, Kansas, Oklahoma, and Nebraska, and the western states, Arizona, California, Colorado, and Montana.

FOUNDATION: Male: The stallions were of Arab, Barb, and Turk blood. They were landed in North America by Spanish explorers, the Conquistadores, and later by Spanish traders. Many became freed to roam the plains of the south and southwest, either by conquest, theft, or voluntary release by their Spanish owners. They crossed and recrossed with mares of the Indian tribes and two distinct strains evolved:

1. The Choctaw, originating in the area of Florida.
2. The Chickasaw, originating in the area of Texas.

Female: The mares were brought to North America by the English. In 1620, the English settlers landed 20 mares at Jamestown, Virginia. They were more or less of the blood lines of the horse of the East—Arab, Barb, and Turk. From these mares, when crossed with Chickasaw stallions and Choctaw stallions, evolved a new type of horse, a family, the Quarter Horse. It was firmly established as a breed by the year 1665 and became the first American breed of horses.

Lest the reader be mistaken in the origin of the Quarter Horse—as was the writer for several years—it does not stem from the English Thoroughbred *tail-male* as does the American Thoroughbred. The Quarter Horse was established from a quarter century to a half century before the arrival in England of the founders of the Thoroughbred family, the Darley Arabian, the Godolphin Arabian, and the Byerly Turk, from whose loins Thoroughbreds evolved.

The Quarter Horse was initially developed for general and utilitarian purposes but, when found to possess unusual and exceptional speed for short distances, he was also used as a running steed by the Colonists. Hence he at first was prominently known as a Quarter Running Horse.

As the Colonies expanded and courses and tracks of larger size were laid out, interest turned to the English Thoroughbred for a longer-distance flat, hurdle, and steeplechase racing steed and also a hunting steed. The Quarter Horse then moved southwest and to the West with the frontiersmen, where they found and perhaps fixed a lasting place for themselves.

Although without a formal association, club, or society for recording and registering the breed until the year 1940, 275 years after it was established in Virginia, a number of choice specimens of both sexes were held apart through a century and a half. By selective breeding, their prepotency has developed several family strains or family blood lines that transmit through their progeny characteristics identifiable and classifiable according to purpose.

The family blood lines as charted in *Ride a Quarter Horse, A Compilation of Standard Characteristics and General Information Pertaining to the Famous Quarter Horse Breed,* published by the American Quarter Horse Association, have been alphabetized by families, and they follow: 1. Old Billy; 2. Blake; 3. Cold Dick; 4. Old Fred; 5. Little Joe; 6. Peter McCue; 7. Printer; 8. Roan Dick; 9. Rondo; 10. Shiloh; 11. Steel Dust; 12. Traveler.

In the year 1940 when the American Quarter Horse Association was organized at Fort Worth, Texas, only 347 horses were registered. At the close of 1954 a total of 81,330 had been registered; as of January 1959 the total accumulated registrations aggregated 134,080— a truly remarkable record spanning two decades of the breed and a tribute to the Association and its *Registry* (*Stud Book*).

Characteristics

COLOR: Bay, black, brown, chestnut, dun, golden, gray, roan, and sorrel.

Albino, Appaloosa, Pinto, and also those with white markings on the underline are ineligible for registration. Those sired by other than registered Quarter Horses are ineligible for registration.

SIZE: Height varies from fourteen two (14.2) hands to fifteen two (15.2) hands. Weight varies from 950 pounds to 1,200 pounds.

OTHER CHARACTERISTICS: The head of the Quarter Horse reflects alertness and intelligence: short and broad and topped by little fox-like ears. Quarter Horses have wide-set kindly eyes, large sensitive nostrils, and short muzzles. Their well-developed jaws indicate great strength. The head is set on the neck at a forty-five-degree angle, with a distinct space between the jawbone and neck muscles. This permits them to work with a low straight-line head. Their medium-length, slightly arched full neck blends into sloping shoulders with medium-high but sharp withers.

Quarter Horses are deep and broad-chested, with a large heart girth and wide-set forelegs blending into their shoulders. Their smooth joints and very short cannons are set on clean fetlocks and medium-length pasterns are supported on well-rounded, well-shaped, concave sound feet of medium size. Their backs are closely coupled, that is, short, and especially powerful. The barrel is formed of deep, well-sprung ribs and the underline runs straight back to the flank. The hind quarters are broad, deep, strong, and well muscled through the thighs, stifles, and gaskins, on down to the hocks. The legs, both front and rear, are flat, firm-boned, and free of fleshiness, puffs, or other blemishes. They dip sharply from croup to tail, an attribute which, with hind legs well muscled both inside and outside, permits fast starting, turning, pivoting, stopping, and also holding.

Quarter Horses have exceedingly good collected and determined action; their starting or getaway, turning, pivoting, stopping, and holding are unequaled in ease of performance, grace, and balance.

Principal Uses

Stock handling; cutting, herding, roping, range riding, and the like.

Show and rodeo competition classes; cutting, working cow horses, reining, hazing, barrel racing, and the like.

Racing over straightaways and circular tracks at limited distances.

Endurance trials, parade mounts, and also pleasure riding, generally under Western tack.

Registry

The American Quarter Horse Association, 2736 West Tenth Street, Amarillo, Texas.

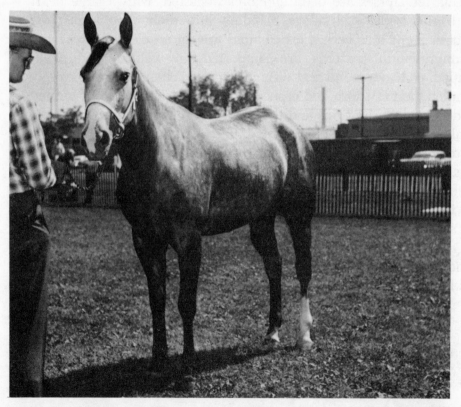

Cricket Dowdy, Mare   Dam: Jackey Adair
Sire: Super Matador   By: King George

Owner: Mr. Peter J. Teller, Middletown, New York.

Caillet's King, Horse   Rider: Robert Burton
   Sire: King

Owner: Mr. W. D. Dana, Healdsburg, California.

Joe Queen, Horse
Sire: Joe E. II

Dam and Sire: Not Furnished

Joe Queen, Horse
Sire: Joe E. II

Jockey: Robert Ford

Trainer: Dallas Clark

Owner: Mr. Audie Murphy, Vail, Arizona.

Curtiss Friscoe Pete, Stallion
Sire: Exline Dapples

Dam: King's X Donna
By: Silver King X

Owner: Fernwood Farm, Mr. and Mrs. A. C. Buehler, Barrington, Illinois.

Shetland

Dainty Doll, Mare   Dam and Sire: Not Furnished
    Sire: Silver Moonlight

Owner: Mr. Clark McKelvey, Euliss, Texas.

Shetland Pony

Origin

PLACE OF ORIGIN: Shetland Islands, 200 miles from the northern coast of Scotland.

FOUNDATION: The original foundation stock of the Shetland Pony is somewhat obscure in history. They probably spring from the small hardy horses of the Roman occupation of England during the fourth and early fifth centuries. When the Romans withdrew in 410 A.D., many of their horses were left behind. Some migrated to the mountainous regions of the mainland areas and others are believed to have migrated to the small bleak reaches of the Shetland Islands. It is not clear, but apparently few if any horses of the different breeds or strains that arrived on the mainland of England in later years were taken or migrated to the Shetland Islands. Thus the intermixing of the small hardy horses there with other blood is of limited extent, if any.

Through many, many years these small horses existed in mountainous terrain almost barren of edible grass and foliage and without man-provided shelter. They became smaller and smaller, but the need of survival through this rugged existence developed self-reliance and they became increasingly hardier, sounder, and smarter, with almost human qualities and personalities. The prepotency and rare qualities of these small horses is imprinted in the pedigrees of the modern-day Shetland Ponies.

Small horses with ponylike characteristics inhabited the mountains of southern Europe in antiquity. These are depicted in Spanish pictures of the Middle Ages. It is possible and probable, it is sometimes said, that some of these were taken or somehow made their way to the Shetland Islands and were the forerunners of present-day Shetland Ponies. The writer, however, prefers the version that present-

137

day Shetland Ponies stem from the small hardy horses of the Roman occupation of England.

There are now three principal or distinct types of Shetland Ponies:

1. The riding type. They are frequently shown under saddle by children, but are best known for children's riding and driving and as companions and family pets.
2. The road type. They are, to a large extent, utilized for showing in harness: single, pairs, tandems, and foursomes. They are also exhibited in six-pony hitches and eight-pony hitches.
3. The draft type resembling a small draft horse. They are used for light hauling and carrying pack loads of peat, firewood, etc. Shetlands are used in England and Wales in coal mining, as their tiny size and sturdiness make them ideal pit ponies.

Five dominant and prominent Shetland Pony strains of the present day in the United States and Canada are:

1. King Larigo; 2. Greyhound; 3. Patton; 4. Prince of Wales; 5. Silver Crescent.

The last named is by Orloff, from whom stem most, if not all silver-dappled Shetlands. The top individuals of these strains are in great demand and a few have sold at public auction up to $50,000.

Characteristics

COLOR: Bay, black, brown, chestnut, cream, dun, gray, roan, mixed (spotted); bay and white, black and white, brown and white, and silver dappled. Most have long flowing silky manes and tails, with their tails brushing the ground.

SIZE: Heights up to 46 inches (46"). It is the outside limit permitted for registration or showing in classes of the breed in the United

States. In Canada the outside limit in show classes is 44 inches (44″).
Weight varies from 250 pounds to 500 pounds.

OTHER CHARACTERISTICS: Most Shetlands are born gentle, from living
with people and with other animals in their native habitat for over a
thousand years.

Exceptionally docile, intelligent, tractable, and the ultimate ideal
for children to ride and drive and as family pets.

They are hardy, sound, sure-footed, and easy keepers, requiring a
minimum of grain and forage to maintain health and good flesh.
They frequently live to a useful life of thirty years and some continue their usefulness to forty years of age.

Principal Uses

Showing under saddle and for general riding and driving by
children.

Showing in harness: single, pairs, tandem; pairs, trios, and foursomes. Also exhibited in six-pony and eight-pony hitches, primarily
as an advertising medium.

Registry

The American Shetland Pony Club, Lafayette, Indiana.

Eight Pony Hitch

Owner: Carolanne Farm, Mr. and Mrs. Oscar Smith, Norfolk, Virginia.

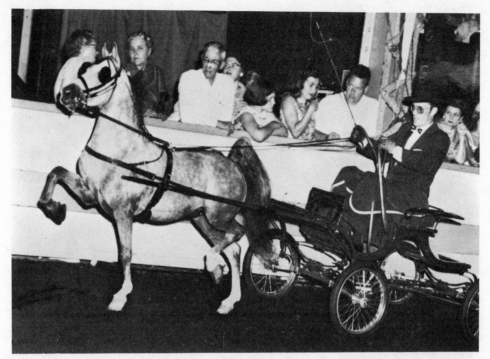

Silver Mane's Meteor Cody, Horse   Driver: Thomas Meeks
   Sire: Silver Mane
              Owner: H. P. Kilkenny & Sons, Cuba City, Wisconsin.

Susie's Miss Boots, Filly (2)   Driver: Miss Susan Scherff
   Sire: Sunset Rhythm's Larry

      Owner: Windy Hollow Farms, Mr. Roger A. Scherff, Frederick, Maryland.

Silver Smoke,
    42″ Shetland

Driver: Mr. G. R. Burrier

Owner: Mr. G. R. Burrier,
            Frederick, Maryland.

Go Boy's Ace, Horse
Sire: Merry Go Boy

Rider: J. B. Smith

Owner: Mrs. G. M. Livingston, New York, New York.

Tennessee Walking Horse

Go Boy's Souvenir, Horse   Rider: Steven Hill
  Sire: Merry Go Boy

Owner: Mr. C. C. Turner, Broadway, Virginia.

Origin

PLACE OF ORIGIN: Tennessee, principally in six of the middle counties, known as the Middle Basin. Now found in all parts of the United States. In recent years, a number have been exported for use on the sugar-cane plantations of Latin and South America.

FOUNDATION: The foundation animals were an admixture of American Saddlebreds, Canadian Pacers, Morgans, Narragansett Pacers (from Rhode Island), Standardbreds, and Thoroughbreds. Horses of these admixtures found their way into Tennessee through the Carolinas, Virginia, and other states, with the settlers who pioneered the settling of the Middle Basin. The history of Tennessee refers to these horses being ridden back and forth between the Carolinas and Tennessee as early as 1790.

The papers of General Andrew Jackson refer to the stallion Free and Easy (whose name derives from his free and easy gait under saddle) being sent to Warren County, North Carolina, for breeding purposes, and also to the stallion Copperbottom, a Canadian Thoroughbred, brought from Kentucky as a colt to North Carolina and thence back to Kentucky and then again to Tennessee as a twenty-year-old, to spend the rest of his life there. Many of the best Tennessee Walkers of today trace to him. He was the founder, while in Kentucky, of the Copperbottom strain of Kentucky saddle horses. Copperbottom's son Morrell's Copperbottom founded the great Slasher family.

Another great early stallion, Traveler (McMeens), was sired by Stump-the-Dealer, a Thoroughbred by Timoleon. Some fifty horses sired by him were in General Edwin Forrest's Cavalry during the War between the States, and not one was lost during the war.

The blood of the pacing strains of Joe Bowers, Brooks, Grey John, Pat Malone, Snow Heels, and the Hals and the Saddlebreds from the

145

Stonewall family that evolved from the Cockspur and Denmark strain left their mark in the propagation of the Tennessee Walking Horse.

During 1935, now a quarter of a century ago, the Tennessee Walking Horse Breeders' Association of America was organized and a breed registry established. Since its organization, registrations have exceeded 50,000. A committee was formed upon its organization to determine a stallion that contributed most to the breed, so as to permit the naming of a foundation sire.

The committee determined, and the association approved, that the foundation sire was Allan, and he became Allan F-1. He was a double-gaited black stallion sired by Allandorf by Onward by George Wilkes by Hambletonian 10, the foundation sire of the American Standardbred. His dam was Maggie Marshall sired by Bradford's Telegraph by Black Hawk by Sherman Morgan, of Narragansett Pacer-Morgan blood.

Allan F-1 late in life had an opportunity through the late J. R. Brantley of Manchester, Tennessee, who purchased him and started the breeding of native mares of good type to him, to produce many horses of renown, but his two outstanding progeny were the stallion Roan Allen F-38 and the mare Merry Legs F-4. Roan Allen F-38 was out of Gertrude F-84, a Denmark mare of saddle breeding, out of a Canadian pacing mare. He was a truly great show horse, ambidextrous to the nth degree, and competed successfully in harness on the trot, at the five gaits of the American Saddlebred, and then at the three gaits of the Tennessee Walker. Roan Allen F-38 in turn sired numerous show winners; the two most outstanding stallions were Merry Boy and Wilson's Allen, each of which established top strains. Merry Legs F-4 was out of Nell Dement F-3, an American Saddlebred mare. She was a truly great show mare and when retired produced thirteen foals, all of them good. Her most famous sons, whose characteristics are much sought after today, are: 1. Bud Allen; 2. Last Change; 3. Major Allen; 4. Merry Boy; and 5. Merry King.

There are many, many others worthy of mention here, but space will not permit further discussion. Lest the reader query the spelling of the name of the foundation sire, ALLAN, as against the spelling of the several progeny that bear his name but with the spelling ALLEN, the writer hastens to state that the spellings are correct and also that the letter F followed by a numeral denotes the family number.

Characteristics

COLOR: Bay, black, brown, chestnut, dun, golden gray, roan, and sorrel. Many of the chestnuts, goldens, roans, and sorrels have white body markings and white legs.

SIZE: Heights vary from fifteen (15.0) hands to sixteen (16.0) hands. Weight varies from 1,000 pounds to 1,200 pounds.

OTHER CHARACTERISTICS: Their three gaits are the flat-footed walk, the running walk, and the canter. By selective breeding the running walk, peculiar to the breed, has become so fixed that it is now considered to be inherited. It is a square four-beat gait with the hind feet overstepping the print of the front feet, with a smooth gliding effect. In its execution the horses bob or nod their heads, some flop their ears, and some snap their teeth in rhythm with the gait's execution. Their canter is executed at a high and rolling movement. Both gaits are easy on the rider. The running walk is easy on the horse, and they can carry it for an extended time and extended distance without distress. The breed is. variously referred to as Tennessee Walkers, Tennessee Plantation Horses, and Tennessee Walking Horses.

Principal Uses

Showing under saddle at a flat-foot walk, running walk, and canter. Rarely, if ever, shown in harness. Extensively used on plantations because of their easy riding gaits. Also used for pleasure riding.

Registry

Tennessee Walking Horse Breeders' Association of America, P. O. Box 87, Lewisburg, Tennessee.

Midnight Mystery, Mare   Rider: Winston Wiser
    Sire: Midnight Sun

Owner: Mr. and Mrs. John H. Amos, Franklin, Tennessee.

Sun's Big Shot, Stallion

Sire: Midnight Sun

Dam: Josie R.

By: Major Bowes

Owner: Mrs. G. M. Livingston, New York, New York.

Merry Go Boy, Stallion   Dam: Wiser's Dimples
  Sire: Merry Boy   By: Giovanni

   Owners: Mr. C. C. Turner, Broadway, Virginia, and Mr. S. W. Beech, Jr., Lewisburg,
   Tennessee.

Brierwood Honey, Mare   Dam: Brierwood Treacle
Sire: Brierwood Mistwyn   By: Welsh Book

Owner: Crefeld Welsh Pony Farm, Mr. George A. Fernley, Plymouth Meeting,
Pennsylvania.

Welsh Mountain Pony

Imp. Farnley Sirius, Stallion   Dam: Imp. Coed Coch Seren
    Sire: Coed Coch Blyndwr   By: Grove Sharp Shooter
        Owner: Farnley Farm, Mrs. J. H. Mackay-Smith, White Post, Virginia.

Welsh Mountain Pony

Origin

PLACE OF ORIGIN: Great Britain, in the Welsh Mountains.

FOUNDATION: The foundation stock of the Welsh Mountain Pony is somewhat obscure in history. They probably spring from the small hardy horses of the Roman occupation during the fourth and early fifth centuries. When the Romans withdrew in 410 A.D., many were left to fend for themselves in the Welsh Mountains. These later crossed with Spanish Andalusians and Barbs and also with the imported Arab, Barb, and Turk stallions of the East and Middle East and small horses of pony characteristics evolved, later designated Welsh Mountain Ponies.

Both the Roman horses and the horses from Spain, the East, and the Middle East were animals considerably larger than the admixture that became the Welsh Mountain Pony. Their decrease in size is attributable to the rugged existence in their habitat in the Welsh Mountains. Roaming in penetratingly cold climate and rugged terrain, without aid or assistance from man, subsisting on whatever could be found among the crags and crannies, they became smaller and smaller throughout the years. In their battle with the elements and their environment for survival, they while decreasing in size increased in stature in its broadest sense. They acquired an unbelievably hardy ruggedness and soundness, exceptional self-reliance, and an almost human personality, qualities that may be equaled by other breeds but certainly not exceeded.

During the nineteenth century and into the twentieth century, improvement in the action, beauty, and symmetry of the breed was obtained by infusion of Arab, Hackney, and Thoroughbred blood. Stallions of these admixtures were directly crossed or were freed to cross with several feral or roving and undomesticated herds. The

153

introduction of alien blood undoubtedly improved the breed; however, it should be understood in largest measure that it was obtained principally through intelligent selection from within the breed.

Private records of the lineage or blood lines of the Welsh Mountain Pony extend back sixty years or more, and a *Registry* (*Stud Book*) formally establishing the breed was published in 1903. A number of males have imprinted their prepotency and precocity in the pedigrees of modern-day Welsh Mountain Ponies. The alphabetized listing below is of those that immediately come to mind. It is not intended to be complete; however, it is hoped that it may be of interest to readers: 1. Bledfa; 2. Brierwood Mistwyn; 3. Brierwood Popwood; 4. Coed Coch Madog; 5. Coed Coch Meilyr; 6. Coed Coch Glyndwr; 7. Dyoll Starlight; 8. Eiddwen; 9. Farnley Sirius; 10. Flyer; 11. Revel Brightlight; 12. Shooting Star.

Characteristics

COLOR: Bay, black, brown, chestnut, cream, dun, gray (the most common), and roan. Piebald and skewbald colorings are excluded. Blazes are common and also white socks and stockings, especially among the lighter colors, the chestnuts, creams, duns, and grays.

SIZE: Height ranges from 43 inches (43″) to 50 inches (50″). The latter is the outside limit permitted for registration and also for qualification for show classes of the breed. Usually there is not much variation in height, as most are between 46 inches (46″) and 48 inches (48″). Weight ranges from 450 pounds to 600 pounds.

OTHER CHARACTERISTICS: Docile, intelligent, tractable, and versatile to the nth degree; hence they are ideal children's mounts and thrive on youthful companionship.

They are hardy, spirited but gentle, with unusual endurance and subsist in good flesh and health on a minimum of grain and forage.

Welsh Ponies are endowed with small shapely heads, tapering muzzles, large wide-set eyes, full open nostrils, and very small pointed ears. They have clean-cut throat latch, lengthy neck set on exceptionally good withers and shoulders, running to a well-coupled (short) back and loins with a deep girth and well-sprung ribs.

Their hind quarters are lengthy, not "cobby" nor "goose-rumped," with the tail bone at a near-horizontal position. They also have a naturally high and gaily waving tail, especially when competing or at play.

Their four-square set-on legs have short, flat cannon bones, flexible tendons, well-developed muscular control, and are carried on particularly small, concave, and sound feet.

Welsh Mountain Pony action is typically forceful and strong, ground-covering; quick, free, and straight from the shoulder in front. In their hind action, the hocks are well flexed in propelling the hind legs well under the body, in a powerful straight-line thrust.

Principal Uses

Showing in harness and under saddle, the latter principally by youngsters. Showing in hand and in breeding classes.

Pleasure riding, fox hunting, stock handling, miniature parade mounts, and jumping. They are noted, in fact are famous, as children's open jumpers.

Registry

The Welsh Pony Society of America, Wicomico Church, Virginia.

Coed Coch Meilyr, Stallion   Dam: Coed Coch Mefusen
Sire: Tregoyd Starlight   By: Coed Coch Glyndwr

Owner: Crefeld Welsh Pony Farm, Mr. George A. Fernley, Plymouth Meeting, Pennsylvania.

Imp. Coed Coch Pelen, Mare and Foal   Dam of Mare: Coed Coch Pioden
Sire: Tregoyd Starlight   Sire of Foal: Liseter Bright Light

Owner: Liseter Hall Farm, Mrs. J. Austin du Pont, Newton Square, Pennsylvania.

Coed Coch Siaradus, Mare
Sire: Coed Coch Glyndwr

and Coed Coch Sulgwyn
Sire: Not Furnished

Dam: Coed Coch Sirius
By: Imp. Bowlder Brightlight

Owner: Coed Coch Stud, Miss M. Brodrick,
Albergele, North Wales.

Gretton Sunlight, Mare
Sire: Bowlder Blue Boy

Dam: Gretton Sunshine
By: Not Furnished

Owner: Ardmore Stud, Mrs. G. D. Rockwell,
King, Ontario, Canada.

Liseter Bright Light, Stallion
Sire: Imp. William (Stormy Weather)

Dam: Farnley Fairlight
By: Imp. Bowlder Brightlight

Owner: Liseter Hall Farm,
Mrs. J. Austin du Pont,
Newton Square, Pennsylvania.

Liseter Shooting Star, Stallion
Sire: Imp. Farnley Morningstar

Dam: Farnley Fairlight
By: Imp. Bowlder Brightlight

Owner: Liseter Hall Farm, Mrs. J. Austin du Pont, Newton Square, Pennsylvania.

Gretton Sunbeam, Mare
Sire: Revel Brightlight

Dam: Gretton Sunshine
By: Dragon

Owner: Crefeld Welsh Pony Farm, Mr. George A. Fernley, Plymouth Meeting, Pennsylvania.

Titan Hanover, Stallion, (3) 1:58   Dam: Tisma Hanover
   Sire: Calumet Chuck, (2) 2:04   By: Peter the Brewer, 2:02 1/2

Owner: Arden Homestead Stable, Goshen, New York.

Standardbred

Novelle Hanover and Twin Foals   Sire of Foals: Galophone, 1:58 1/5
  Sire: Hoot Mon, (3) 2:00

Owner: Clearview Stable, Mr. Norman S. Woolworth, Winthrop, Maine.

Standardbred

Origin

PLACE OF ORIGIN: United States, principally Orange County, New York.

FOUNDATION: The foundation sire was Hambletonian 10 (Rysdyk's Hambletonian) sired by Abdallah by Messenger, and his dam was the Charles Kent mare by Bellfounder, a Norfolk Trotter from England. The foundation mares were Cleveland Bays, Hackneys, Morgans, and other native mares of trotting proclivity.

Messenger, the grandsire of Hambletonian 10, was a gray Thoroughbred imported from England, successful on the running turf and as a progenitor of outstanding Thoroughbreds and Trotters. Messenger was the forerunner of the present-day Standardbreds in America.

The first accepted harness racing record was established by the trotting gelding Yankee at 2:59 for a mile at Harlem, New York, during 1806. The fastest present-day trotting record was established by the gray gelding Greyhound at 1:55 1/4 for a mile at Lexington, Kentucky, during 1938. The fastest present-day pacing records were established by, first, the free-legged bay stallion Billy Direct, at 1:55 for a mile at Lexington, Kentucky, during 1938, and second, the *hobbled* brown stallion Adios Harry at 1:55 for a mile in a race at Vernon, New York, during 1955.

The greatest racing campaigner of all time is "the immortal" brown free-legged pacing stallion Dan Patch, who traces twenty-two times to the Thoroughbred, Imp. Messenger. No other Standardbred has approached him, certainly not a free-legged one. The bay colt Meadow Al, (2) 2:00 3/5, (3) 2:00 2/5h, looms as a potential successor. (A small "h" following a record indicates that the record was made on a track one-half mile in circumference. A half-mile track is some three seconds slower than a mile track.)

Meadow Al is now a four-year-old. He set a number of records at two and at three and it is anticipated that he will continue to race brilliantly.

There is much in the press, over the air, and in conversation about which racing horse has earned the largest amount of money. Dan Patch's earnings from purses and exhibitions aggregated in excess of $3 millions. The exact amount was never precisely tallied, however; the foregoing amount was released officially many years ago by the late Marion W. Savage, then the owner of Dan Patch. It has never been challenged because of the forthright honesty of Mr. Savage.

Dan Patch was foaled on April 28, 1896, at Oxford, Indiana, the property of the late Daniel Messener. He was sold during 1900 to the late M. E. Sturgis of New York, New York, and then later was sold to the late Marion W. Savage of Minneapolis, Minnesota. He died on July 14, 1916, at the age of twenty, at Mr. Savage's International Stock Farm at Savage, Minnesota. On the following day, July 15, 1916, Mr. Savage passed away.

During his training, racing, and exhibiting career he was handled by three men: first by the late John Wattles, second by the late Myron McHenry, and third by the late Harry C. Hersey for seven years, from 1903 to 1909 inclusive. He campaigned for ten years, racing or exhibiting, from 1900 to 1909 inclusive. He was barred from racing during 1903 because of the lack of worthy competitors. He established more world's records than any other racing performer and he paced more fast miles than any other harness racing performer. His world's records included:

Over a Mile Track

One mile in 1:55 1/4, one mile in 1:55 (not officially accepted by the record association), one mile to four-wheel wagon in 1:57 1/4,* one mile to high wheel sulky (wooden wheels and rims with iron tires) in 2:04 3/4, and one-half mile in 56 seconds—both of these on the same day—and two miles in 4:17.*

Over a Half-Mile Track

One mile in 2:01 and one mile to four-wheel wagon in 2:05.*

During his career he paced one mile in 1:55, one mile in 1:55 1/4, two miles in 1:56, three miles in 1.56 1/4, and his fast miles averaged fourteen in 1:56 1/2, thirty in 1:57 1/2, forty-five in 1:58, seventy-three in 1:59 1/2, and one hundred and twenty in 2:02 1/2.

The records on Dan Patch are incomplete because of his being barred from racing. It is, therefore, necessary to refer to harness racing journals for his numerous exhibition performances throughout the length and breadth of the United States. A perusal of those sources indicates that he started no less than one hundred and thirty-four times, sixty-one in racing mile heats, winning fifty-eight thereof. In addition to his strenuous training and campaigning over a period of ten years, he was in stud during seven of those years and served from fifty to seventy mares in each breeding season. He sired numerous harness racing performers, of which one hundred and thirty-eight pacers and thirty-eight trotters obtained standard (official) records.

As a wind-up to the above brief recitation of the career of this phenomenal performer, the following verbatim statement made to the writer by his late handler, Harry C. Hersey, follows:

Dan Patch set his official mark of 1:55 1/4 at Lexington, Kentucky, during 1905. . . . It was at the same track during 1908 that he came close to setting the miraculous time of 1:54, or better. . . . He was at the three-quarter pole in 1:25, speed such as had never been heard of or ever dreamed of before. . . . At that point Cobweb [the running horse setting the pace] hemorrhaged and slowed up; before I could pull Dan out to go, precious seconds were lost. . . . Notwithstanding that mishap he finished out in 1:56 1/4, with the last quarter in only 31 1/4 seconds. . . . Dan could, and always did, close out his fast miles

*Present world's records.

in 29 seconds or better, hence such a quarter (which I believe him fully capable of) would have resulted in a mile in 1:54; perhaps he would have shaded that.

A listing of the truly great harness racing performers of the twentieth century would fill a book to overflowing. The following list is limited to two of each sex, alphabetically, with their best records at one mile:

Trotters

Males: Galophone, 1:58 1/5, and Titan Hanover, (3) 1:58

Mares: Emily's Pride, (3) 1:58, and Rosalind, 1:56 3/4

Geldings: Darn Safe, 1:59, and Greyhound, 1:55 1/4

Pacers, Free-legged

Males: Dan Patch, 1:55 1/4, and Single G, 1:58 1/2

Mares: Countess Adios, (2) 1:59 2/5, (3) 1:57 3/5, and
Margaret Dillon, 1:58 1/4

Geldings: Hollyrood Volo, 2:00 1/4, and Sir Roche, 1:59 1/4

Pacers in Hobbles

Males: Adios Butler, 1:54 3/5, and Good Time, 1:57 4/5

Mares: Bell Acton, 1:58 3/5, and Her Ladyship, 1:56 3/4

Geldings: Little Pat, 1:58 3/4, and Winnipeg, 1:57 3/4

Double-Gaited Champions

	Time		
	Trotting	*Pacing*	*Total*
Stallion:			
Steamin' Demon	1:59 1/5	1:58 4/5	3:58
Mare:			
Calumet Evelyn	1:59 1/2	1:59 1/4	3:58 3/4
Gelding:			
Nate Hanover	2:01 3/4	1:59	4:00 3/4

Characteristics

COLOR: Bay, black, brown, chestnut, dun, gray, roan, sorrel, and now a new color looms. A family of harness racing horses of new color is in the offing as the registered as roan but actually multicolored stallion King Majesty, with a pacing record of 2:10h and a separate timing of 2:07, has sired four foals out of solid-colored mares; three or 75 per cent of the foals have multicolors and variable colorings and hues exceeding those of their sire.

King Majesty was sired by the third or more generation's black stallion, His Majesty, with a pacing record of 1:59 1/2 for a mile. The dam of King Majesty was the fourth or more generation's brown mare Janet Gaynor, a trotter, running to the world's champion sire, Peter Volo, with a four-year-old trotting record of 2:02 for a mile. King Majesty is now fourteen years of age and is still racing near his record over fair half-mile tracks.

The three (of four) multicolored foals by King Majesty appear to be throwbacks, reversion of either atavistic or mutative origin; a biologist or geneticist might be able to determine which. As the American Albino has been determined to have originated atavistically, refer thereto for definition of atavism; and as the Morgan is believed to have originated mutatively, refer thereto for a definition of mutation.

SIZE: Height varies from fourteen (14.0) hands to sixteen (16.0) hands. Weight varies from 900 pounds to 1,150 pounds. Males in the stud (stallions) often weigh up to 1,300 pounds.

OTHER CHARACTERISTICS AND MISCELLANY: Standardbreds are endowed with a high degree of endurance, energy, gameness, intelligence, and over-all quality. The harness racing horses, trotters and pacers, are noted for their ability to race heats (nowadays up to three) to a capacity of their respective speeds, from three-quarters of a mile to a mile and a quarter: some up to a mile and a half.

They are generally ruggeder and plainer in conformation than Thoroughbreds (running horses), from which they stem tail-male.

In recent years, Standardbreds have been piling up Axtell blood in descending line, principally through Axworthy, Guy Axworthy, Dillon Axworthy, Dean Hanover, etc., and Happy Medium blood in descending line, principally through Pilot Medium, Peter the Great, Peter Volo, Volomite, etc., and also Chimes blood, in descending line, principally through The Abbe, Abbedale, Hal Dale, Adios, etc.

A few breeders have returned to the Thoroughbred for mares to cross with Standardbred stallions with the intent and hope that in two or three generations a new line of successful harness racing horses will result. Also, a few breeders have imported French Trotting stallions and Orloff Trotting stallions for crossing with their Standardbred mares.

The Hackney Horse, Morgan Horse, and Tennessee Walking Horse breeds are *closely akin* to the Standardbred breed. Bellfounder, a Norfolk Trotter, was the first imported registered Hackney stallion from England. He is the sire of the Charles Kent mare, the dam of the Standardbred family founder, Hambletonian 10. Justin Morgan, the foundation sire of the Morgan breed, sired, and his descendants have produced, numerous trotters that have successfully competed in harness racing in the United States and Canada. Allan F-1, the foundation sire of the Tennessee Walking Horse, was also a double-gaited pacer and trotter. He was sired by Allandorf, by Onward, by George Wilkes, by Hambletonian 10, the Standardbred family founder.

The Hackney's "high going" is the result of selective breeding and training, and it is "upped" by the use of heavy shoes and feet of extended length (high heels and long toes). When out of training and barefooted or in slippers (slippers are light-weight flat shoes or half-shoes, sometimes called tips), they return to a normal walk and trot movement. The Morgans are trained and raced (in harness and under saddle), shown, and worked in light-weight flat shoes with normal angle and medium-length feet. The Tennessee Walking Horse's high going, especially at the running walk (an amble or pacelike gait) is the result of selective breeding and training and is "upped" a bit by the use of heavy shoes and extended-length feet. When out of training and barefooted or in slippers, they return to a normal walk and trot movement.

These three breeds have demonstrated competitive class, year in and year out, for many years. It would appear that carefully selected Hackney, Morgan, and Tennessee Walking mares would be ideal outcrosses for producing harness racing horses: Hackney and Morgan mares for producing trotters, and Tennessee Walking mares for producing pacers.

Principal Uses

Racing in harness as trotters and pacers. Showing in harness as bike horses and roadsters.

Some have the conformation and finish to compete in the show ring in fine harness classes against American Saddlebred Horses, Hackney Horses, and others.

Some are used for general work in certain areas. A few are used for riding mounts but generally they are not considered better than fair, because of their carriage and rather low long-striding gait.

Registry

United States Trotting Association, 1349 East Broad Street, Columbus, Ohio.

Galophone, Stallion, 1:58 1/5 &
     2:00 1/5h
   Sire: Bill Gallon, 1:59 1/5

Dam: Carophone, 2:12 4/5h
By: Phonograph, 1:59 1/4

Owner: Walnut Hall Stud, Donerail, Kentucky.

Hickory Smoke, Colt, (2) 2:03 1/5   Driver: John A. Simpson
                    (3) 2:00 1/5, 2:01 2/5h
    Sire: Titan Hanover, (3) 1:58

Hickory Smoke, Stallion, 1:58 2/5   Dam: Misty Hanover, 2:08 3/5h
    Sire: Titan Hanover, (3) 1:58   By: Dean Hanover, (3) 1:58 1/2

        Owner: Hanover Shoe Farms, Inc., Hanover, Pennsylvania.

Star's Pride, Colt, (2) 2:06 2/5, (3) 2:02   Driver: Harry Pownall
   Sire: Worthy Boy, (3) 2:02 1/2

Star's Pride, Stallion, 1:57 1/5   Dam: Star Drift, 2:03
   Sire: Worthy Boy, (3) 2:02 1/2   By: Mr. McElwyn, 1:59 1/4

Owners: Mr. E. Roland Harriman, New York, New York, and Mr. L. B. Sheppard,
   Hanover, Pennsylvania.

Greyhound, Gelding, 1:55 1/4   Driver: S. F. Palin
   Sire: Guy Abbey, (3) 2:06 3/4

Greyhound, Gelding, 2:01 3/4   Rider: Mrs. F. L. Van Lennep
   Sire: Guy Abbey, (3) 2:06 3/4

Owner: Mr. E. J. Baker, St. Charles, Illinois.

Emily's Pride, Filly, (3) 1:58   Driver: Flick Nipe
    Sire: Star's Pride, 1:57 1/5

Owners: Castleton Farm, Lexington, Kentucky, and Walnut Hall Farm, Donerail, Kentucky.

Hickory Pride, Colt, (2) 2:07 2/5   Driver: Delvin A. Miller
                      (3) 2:01 2/5, 2:03 2/5h
    Sire: Star's Pride, 1:57 1/5

Owners: Mr. Bowman A. Brown, Harrisburg, Pennsylvania; Mr. Royal E. Cleveland, Camp Hill, Pennsylvania; and Mr. Max Hempt, Mechanicsburg, Pennsylvania.

Rosalind, Mare, 1:56 3/4   Driver: Benjamin F. White
     Sire: Scotland, 1:59 1/4
              Owner: Mr. Gibson A. White, Lexington, Kentucky.

Greyhound, Gelding, 1:55 1/4   Driver: S. F. Palin   Rosalind, Mare, 1:56 3/4
     Sire: Guy Abbey, (3) 2:06 3/4   Sire: Scotland, 1:59 1/4

Owner: Mr. E. J. Baker,   Owner: Mr. Gibson A. White,
           St. Charles, Illinois.   Lexington, Kentucky.

Titan Hanover, Colt, (2) 2:00   Driver: Harry E. Pownall
  Sire: Calumet Chuck, (2) 2:04

Titan Hanover, Colt, (3) 1:58   Driver: Harry E. Pownall
  Sire: Calumet Chuck, (2) 2:04
          Owner: Arden Homestead Stable, Goshen, New York.

Billy Direct, Horse, 1:55   Driver: Victor Fleming
  Sire: Napoleon Direct, 1:59 3/4

  Owners: Mr. P. J. Downey, Worcester, Massachusetts, and Mr. Daniel McConville, Ogdensburg, New York.

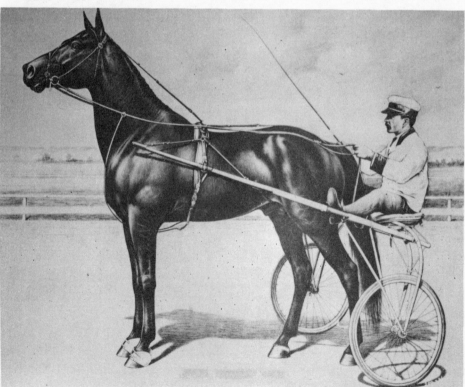

Dan Patch, Horse, 1:55 1/4   Driver: Harry C. Hersey
  Sire: Joe Patchen, 2:02 1/4

  Owner: International Stock Farm, Mr. Marion W. Savage, Minneapolis, Minnesota.

Her Ladyship, Mare, 1:56 3/4   Driver: Dr. Hugh M. Parshall
  Sire: Abbedale, 2:02 1/2

Owner: Mr. E. J. Baker, St. Charles, Illinois.

Meadow War, Horse, 2:02 2/5   Driver: Richard H. Thomas
  Sire: Adios, 1:57 1/5

Owner: Bergstrom Stables, Westbury, New York.

Van Hanover, Colt, (3) 2:02 3/5   Driver: Richard H. Thomas
   Sire: Nibble Hanover, 1:58 3/4

Owner: G-Mac Stable, Massapequa, New York.

Hollyrood Volo, Gelding, 2:00 1/4   Driver: Henry C. Thomas
   Sire: Peter Volo, 2:02

Owners: Mr. C. E. Beveridge, Chicago, Illinois, and Mr. Henry C. Thomas, Springfield, Illinois.

Entrance, Site of "The Hambletonian"
A Stake for Three-Year-Old Trotters

Starting Gate and Field of Three-Year-Old Trotters
The First Heat of "The Hambletonian of 1958,"
Won by Emily's Pride

DuQuoin State Fair Track, DuQuoin, Illinois.

The French Trotter, Jamin, Trotting in 1:58 4/5
DuQuoin State Fair Track, DuQuoin, Illinois.

Grandstand
Historic Track, Goshen, New York.

Trotting Race, Paddock, and Stabling

Finish of Trotting Race

Historic Track, Goshen, New York.

Grandstand and Clubhouse

Trotters Parading to Post

Awaiting a Winner

Saratoga Raceway, Saratoga Springs, New York.

Darn Safe, a Winner
  (World's Record 1:59 4/5h)
   Saratoga Raceway, Saratoga Springs, New York.

An Aerial View of the Plant
   Roosevelt Raceway, Westbury, New York.

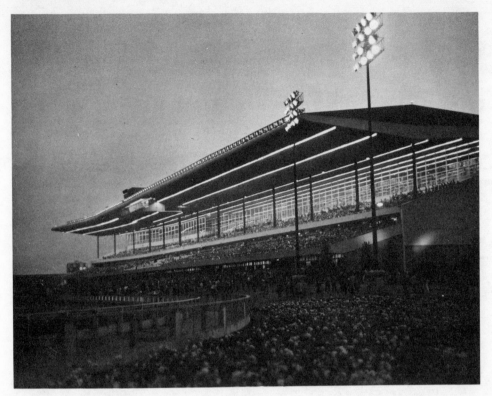

Overflow Night Crowd

Free-Legged Countess Adios (3) Bests Nine Top Colts (In Hobbles).

International Trot, 1960:
 Hairos (Holland), Crevalcore (Italy), and Silver Song (USA)

Roosevelt Raceway, Westbury, New York.

Standardbred Harness Racing—Scandinavia

Down Backstretch, 13 in View

Charlottelund Track, Charlottelund, Denmark.

Around First Turn, 15 in View

Night Scene

Charlottelund Track, Charlottelund, Denmark.

Short Way Around First Turn

Down Stretch First Time Around

   Bjerkebänen Track, Oslo, Norway.

Snow Racing, 11 in View

Bjerkebänen Track, Oslo, Norway.

Parade to Post

Solvälla Track, Stockholm, Sweden.

Six Wide Around First Turn

All Trotting, All in Open Bridles

Solvälla Track, Stockholm, Sweden.

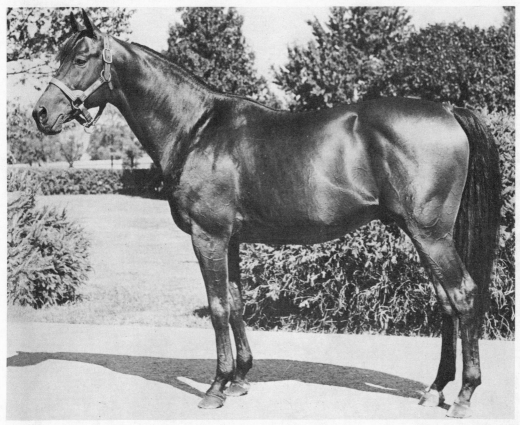

Citation, Stallion
Sire: Bull Lea

Dam: Imp. Hydroplane II
By: Hyperion

Owner: Calumet Farm, Lexington, Kentucky.

Thoroughbred

Paddock, Walking Ring, and Parade to Track
Hialeah Race Course, Hialeah, Florida.

Thoroughbred

Origin

PLACE OF ORIGIN: England and throughout the United States.

FOUNDATION: In England: The tap-root males were of imported Arab, Barb, and Turk blood; the tap-root mares were of the same bloodlines and, in addition, included native mares of Galloway, Highland Dun, Scotch Pony, and numerous others of an admixture going back to the beginning of history. The year 1700 or the beginning of the eighteenth century is the first practical date to account for the Thoroughbred, as it is generally known.

While actually there were many foundation males of Arab, Barb, and Turk blood, the ones most prominently responsible for the evolution of the English Thoroughbred were:

1. The Byerly Turk, a Turk foaled about 1679 and in the stud as late as 1698. The Turks were an admixture of Arab, Persian, and other Asiatic breeds. They were from fifteen (15.0) hands to sixteen (16.0) hands high.
2. The Darley Arabian, an Arab foaled in 1699, arriving in England in 1704, and in the stud as late as 1734. He stood about fifteen (15.0) hands high.
3. The Godolphin Arabian, an Arab, foaled about 1724. He stood about fifteen (15.0) hands high; some say fourteen three (14.3) hands high.
   NOTE: Some authorities claim the Godolphin Arabian was a Barb.
4. The Alcock Arabian, an Arab, brought to England during the reign of Queen Anne, 1702-1714. He was a gray, and he seems to be responsible for the gray color of virtually all present-day Thoroughbreds although some grays also trace in unbroken sequence of grays to the Brownlow Turk.

191

Early English breeders found Arab blood constituted an excellent cross with Barb blood and Turk blood, as from the Arab was produced speed, stoutness, and stride; from the Barb was produced length; and from the Turk was produced height.

The reader should be informed, however, that the early history in England of the Arab, Barb, and Turk is somewhat vague. For a great part, they were prizes of war and were acquired in various Middle East and Asiatic countries. They were designated by the area from which they were secured but may have arrived there from another area. That is, a horse acquired from Arabia was designated an Arab, a horse acquired in Turkey was designated a Turk, and an Arab acquired in Spain or Barbary (northern coast of Africa) was likely to be designated a Barb. As the difference between the three breeds was limited, the individuals could not be identified beyond question. The true or so-called pure Arabian, however, came from Arabia and Egypt where the Arab breed was cultivated and nurtured for many centuries.

In America the tap-roots, male and female, that have persisted have in point of fact a better foundation, better known sources, than those of the English tap-roots because by 1750 the Thoroughbred was a well-established breed. The sires of American mares, for the most part, were from imported stallions of known ancestry and merit rather than from unidentified Arabs, Barbs, and Turks. Better mares were also available for import from England from the year 1750 on. It should be understood by the reader, however, that all American tap-root mares were not from imported racing animals; most of them were, but some came from lower sources and many of these have proved invaluable in the American Thoroughbred Horse.

In America (as elsewhere) all male lines stem from Eclipse, great-great-grandson of the Darley Arabian; Herod, great-great-grandson of the Byerly Turk; and Matchem, grandson of the Godolphin Arabian. The foundation of the Thoroughbred, for the most part, consisted in selective breeding: the breeding of imported stallions to imported mares or good-quality native mares. In turn the daughters of such mares were bred either to other imported stallions, sons of such stallions, or male line descendants that had demonstrated merit, with the result that the native blood has been obscured by the imported blood. Cold blood remaining in the American Thoroughbred or the English Thoroughbred is so far back in the pedigree that it is considered negligible.

The first Thoroughbred importations into America were *Bully Rock or Bulle Rock in 1730, *Spark and the mare *Queen Mab in 1745-1747, *Traveller (Morton's) in 1748, in 1750 the mare *Selima, an outstanding racer and one of the most distinguished and lasting sources in American pedigrees, and in 1755 *Othello and later *Janus and *Fearnought. Then later in 1788 came the successful gray racer *Messenger, to become the most illustrious and renowned progenitor of racing horses of all time. With equal facility he sired the best performers of the running turf and the trotting turf. He is the grandsire of unbeaten American Eclipse and also the distinguished Duroc. The former at nine years of age, carrying 127 pounds, won three heats over the great four-year-old Sir Henry carrying 108 pounds on May 23, 1823 over the Union Course, Long Island, New York, for the then unheard-of stupendous sum of $40,000. The latter, Duroc, sired innumerable performers of distinction and many present-day American Thoroughbreds trace to him. Messenger was also the grandsire of Hambletonian 10, the Standardbred family founder, to which trace over 90 per cent of present-day harness horses in America. Unquestionably Messenger is entitled to the accolade of the greatest of the great horses known to man.

Racing in America between Thoroughbred horses with pedigrees had its beginning at Annapolis, Maryland during 1745.

In New York, where horses arrived as early as 1625, there was racing on Long Island as far back as 1665, probably with horses of Flemish origin. Early papers also record racing in the Carolinas during 1734, in Virginia during 1739, and in Maryland during 1745; these were informally staged and do not have official records.

* = Imported.

The *American Stud Book* was begun by Sanders D. Bruce in 1873. It was purchased in 1896 by The Jockey Club; all American registrations are now recorded in it.

A listing of the truly great racing performers in America during this century would overflow a book of this size. Limiting the number to two by sex alphabetically are these:

Males: Citation and Man O' War

Mares: Gallorette and Twilight Tear

Geldings: Armed and Exterminator

A wave of protesting letters may be the result, unless the writer also recognizes the following as truly great—males: Assault, Bally Ache, Nashua, Native Dancer, Noor, Round Table, Seabiscuit, Stymie, Swaps, Tom Fool, and Tompion; among the mares: Black Helen, Idun, Regret, Royal Native, and Top Flight; geldings, separated as to flat racing: Delegate, Donor, Joe Jones, Let's Dance, Lucky Draw, Marriage, Sarazen, Social Outcast, and Teamaker; and steeplechasing: Ancestor, Elkridge, and Neji.

Characteristics

COLOR: Bay, black, brown, chestnut, gray, and occasionally roan. Some have prominent white markings on the head and legs; however, few have head markings with sufficient white to be termed bald or bald-faced.

SIZE: Height varies from fifteen (15.0) hands to seventeen (17.0) hands. Weight varies from 900 pounds to 1,200 pounds, in training. Males in the stud (stallions) weigh up to 1,300 pounds.

OTHER CHARACTERISTICS: Thoroughbreds possess a high degree of endurance, energy, gameness, quality, and refinement. They generally have a long muscular frame, a deep strong chest set high on the withers, muscular, well-set legs with fairly long pasterns and sound feet.

Males are freely used to improve other light breeds in the United States and the native unregistered mares in Mexico and Latin America. In recent years, in the United States, a few Harness Horse breeders have returned to the purchase of Thoroughbred mares for breeding to Standardbred stallions with the intent and hope that, within two or three generations, good if not exceptional harness racing horses will result. Jamin, the truly great harness racing champion of France (American Record 1:58 4/5 for a mile) has for his third dam Gainsborough Girl, by the Thoroughbred stallion, Gainsborough.

Principal Uses

Racing on the flat (dirt), turf (grass), hurdles (hedge), and steeplechasing (fences, brooks, etc.). Polo playing, hunting, jumping; in the field and at horse shows. Also for pleasure riding, high school performance, dressage, and some stock handling and as rodeo performers.

They are rarely driven for pleasure or in the show ring. Many are used as running prompters, hitched to a bike cart, for harness horses; in exhibition performances and for the education of young horses to perform at speed.

Registry

The Jockey Club, 300 Park Avenue, New York, New York.

Bold Ruler, Colt (3)   Jockey: Edward Arcaro
    Sire: Imp. Nasrullah

Bold Ruler, Colt (3)   Jockey: Edward Arcaro
    Sire: Imp. Nasrullah   Trainer: James E. Fitzsimmons

Owner: Wheatley Stable, Old Westbury, New York.

Bold Ruler, Stallion
  Sire: Imp. Nasrullah

Dam: Miss Disco
By: Discovery

Owner: Wheatley Stable, Old Westbury, New York.   Trainer: James E. Fitzsimmons

Citation, Colt (3)
  Sire: Bull Lea

Jockey: Edward Arcaro

Owner: Calumet Farm, Lexington, Kentucky.

Citation, Colt (3)   Jockey: Edward Arcaro
Sire: Bull Lea   Trainer: Horace E. Jones
Owner: Calumet Farm, Lexington, Kentucky.

Uncle Miltie, Colt (2)   Jockey: David Gorman
Sire: Heather Broom
Owner: Point-A-View Stud Farm, Yardley, Pennsylvania; Mr. Joseph J. Colando,
Maywood, New Jersey.

Uncle Miltie, Colt (3)
Sire: Heather Broom

Jockey: Hedley Woodhouse
Trainer: Dr. A. C. Colando, D.V.S.

Uncle Miltie, Stallion
Sire: Heather Broom

Dam: Twink-Mo
By: Mokatim

Owner: Point-A-View Stud Farm, Yardley, Pennsylvania; Mr. Joseph J. Colando, Maywood, New Jersey.

Capot, Colt (3)
Sire: Menow

Owner: Greentree Stable,
Manhasset, New York.

Coaltown, Horse
Sire: Bull Lea

Owner: Calumet Farm,
Lexington, Kentucky.

Nashua, Colt (3)
   Sire: Imp. Nasrullah

Owner: Belair Stud,
   Bowie, Maryland.

Tom Fool, Colt (3)
   Sire: Menow

Owner: Greentree Stable,
   Manhasset, New York.

Jockey: Theodore Atkinson

Aerial View

Main Entrance
Aqueduct Race Course, Aqueduct, New York.

On the Way to Paddock

Outdoor Paddock, Walking Area, and Grandstand
Aqueduct Race Course, Aqueduct, New York.

Start of Race
  Aqueduct Race Course, Aqueduct, New York.

Grandstand, Infield, and Hurdle Race

  Belmont Park Race Course, Elmont, New York.

Spectators and Finish of Race
   Belmont Park Race Course, Elmont, New York.

Around the Turn
   Saratoga Race Course, Saratoga Springs, New York.

Into the Stretch — Saratoga Race Course, Saratoga Springs, New York.
The New York Racing Association, Inc., New York, New York.

Starting Gate and Start of Race
Monmouth Park Race Course, Oceanport, New Jersey.

Clubhouse and Race Around First Turn

Grandstand and Finish of Race

Monmouth Park Race Course, Oceanport, New Jersey.

A Photo Finish

Monmouth Park Race Course, Oceanport, New Jersey.

Clubhouse and Grandstand: Rear View and Walking Ring

Parade to Post

Gulf Stream Park Race Course, Hallandale, Florida.

Grandstand, Infield Lake, and Race at Quarter Pole

Grandstand and Race Around First Turn

Gulf Stream Park Race Course, Hallandale, Florida.

Plant, Aerial View
  Hialeah Race Course, Hialeah, Florida.

Clubhouse and Grandstand, Rear View

Grandstand and Race Around First Turn
  Hialeah Race Course, Hialeah, Florida.

Grandstand, Across the Infield View

Walk-Up Start

Finish: Tudor Era, First; Sailor's Guide, Second; and Ballymoss, Third.
Tudor Era was disqualified and placed second, for impeding Sailor's Guide at the entrance of stretch.

Laurel Race Course, Laurel, Maryland.

Trophy Presentation to the Owners of Sailor's Guide, Mr. and Mrs. Keith Dibb and Mr. A. C. (Bert) Dibb of Australia, by Governor Theodore McKeldin of Maryland; J. Bowes Bond, Trainer of Sailor's Guide; and Mr. John D. Schapiro, President of Laurel Race Course

Laurel Race Course, Laurel, Maryland.

Thoroughbred Racing—Cuba

Grandstand and Clubhouse

Oriental Park Race Course, Havana (Marianao), Cuba.

Clubhouse Lawn and First Turn
Oriental Park Race Course, Havana (Marianao), Cuba.

Starting Gate and Start of Race

A Mirror Image Finish

A Winner. Marlace With Owner, Friends, Trainer, and Jockey
Oriental Park Race Course, Havana (Marianao), Cuba.

Master William, Gelding   Rider: Mr. Hugh Wiley
Owner: Mrs. Wm. Joshua Barney, Jr., Southport, Connecticut.

United States Equestrian Team

Mr. Wm. C. Steinkraus, Captain, Mr. George Morris, Mr. Hugh Wiley, and "Nautical"

United States Equestrian Team

President
 Mr. Whitney Stone,
 New York, New York

Vice-President
 Mr. Walter B. Devereaux,
 Rye, New York

Executive Vice-President
 and Treasurer
 Brig. Gen. F. W. Boye, USA Ret.,
 Warrenton, Virginia

Secretary
 Mr. A. M. Montgomery,
 Uno, Virginia

Origin and Activities

This is a nonprofit organization devoted to the support and training of teams to represent the United States in the field of International Equestrian Competition.

Joining hands with the Olympic Equestrian Games Committee and the United States Olympic Committee, teams are provided to represent the United States in the Olympic Games and the Pan American Games.

Prior to 1949, the responsibility for representation in international jumping competition was vested in the Cavalry School at Fort Riley, Kansas, an agency of the United States Army. Following the 1948 Olympic Games, the United States Army dissolved its horse cavalry, thereby eliminating the possibility of future international jumping teams being sponsored by it.

Realizing the value of a United States international jumping team, a number of enthusiasts banded together in 1950 to organize and carry on with a civilian team. They formed the International Equestrian Team, Inc., a nonprofit organization, incorporated under the laws of the State of New York. In that year a team was formed and it competes annually at Harrisburg, Pennsylvania, Madison Square Garden, New York, N. Y., and Toronto, Canada. In 1951,

219

better to amplify its name and functions, the name was changed to the United States Equestrian Team, Inc. A year later, in 1952, a team competed in the Olympic Games at Helsinki, Finland. In 1955, a team competed in the Pan American Games at Mexico City, Mexico. In 1956, a team competed in the Olympic Games at Stockholm, Sweden. In 1959, it again appeared at the Pan American Games, held this time in Chicago, Illinois.

In addition to international competition, the team participates in open competition each year throughout the United States, Canada, and various countries in Europe and South America, and members of the team also individually participate in open competition in various outdoor and indoor show circuits.

Address

90 Broad Street, New York 4, N. Y.

Ksar d'Esprit, Gelding   Rider: Mr. Wm. C. Steinkraus

Owner: Miss Eleo Sears, Pride's Crossing, Massachusetts.

Defense, Gelding   Rider: Mr. Frank Chapot

Owner: Miss Peggy Augustus, Old Keswick, Cobham, Virginia.

"Master William," Mr. Hugh Wiley, and "Nautical"

Mr. George Morris, Mr. Bertalan de Nemethy, Coach, and Mr. Frank Capot

Sinjon, Gelding

Rider: Mr. George Morris   Owner: Miss Ellen Dineen, Northport, New York.

Pennsylvania National Horse Show Arena
  State Farm Show Arena Building, Harrisburg, Pennsylvania.

New York National Horse Show Arena
  Madison Square Garden, New York, New York.

Bellwood Horse Show Ring, Bellwood, Pennsylvania

Pennsylvania National Horse Show Arena, State Farm
Show Arena Building, Harrisburg, Pennsylvania.

A Gallery of Miscellany:

New York National Horse Show Arena
Madison Square Garden, New York, New York.

A Favorite Mount: Equestrian, Mr. Arthur Godfrey;
Horse, Catoctin Gold (Goldie)

Owner: Beacon Hill Stables, Mr. and Mrs. Arthur Godfrey, Paeonian Springs,
Virginia.

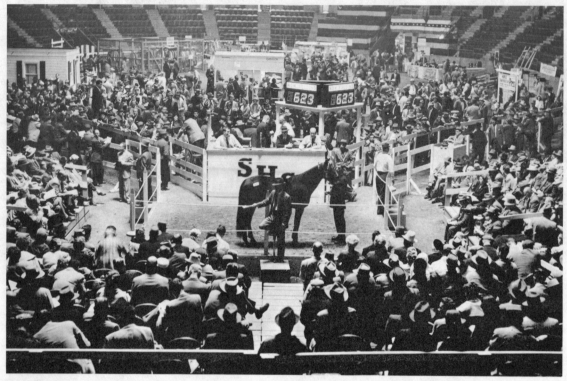

Auction Sale

Standardbred Horse Auction Sales Company, State Farm Show Arena Building,
Harrisburg, Pennsylvania.

Transportation Equipment

   A Horse Van

   A Horse Van, Inside View

A Solid Silver Trophy

Bellaire, Gelding   Rider: Mr. Frank D. Chapot

Owner: Chado Farm, Mr. Frank D. Chapot, Wallpack, New Jersey.

Sinbad, Gelding   Rider: Mr. Frank D. Chapot

Owner: Mrs. Walter B. Devereux, Rye, New York.

Times Square, Gelding   Rider: Mrs. Vernon G. Cardy

Times Square, Gelding   Rider: Mr. Vernon G. Cardy

Owner: Mr. Vernon G. Cardy, St. Marguerite Station, Quebec, Canada.

First Boy, Gelding

Rider: Mr. Wm. C. Steinkraus

Owner: Miss Joan Magid, Mamaroneck, New York.

Polo Playing

American International Polo Team

Members: Mr. Thomas Hitchcock, Jr., Mr. Winston Guest, Mr. Earl A. S. Hopping, and Mr. Eric Pedley

A Game in Progress

A Lost Ball

Blind Brook Polo Club, Purchase, New York.

A Game in Progress

A Player's Spill

Oak Brook Polo Club, Hinsdale, Illinois.

Imp. Katrina

Owner: Mr. Thomas Hitchcock, Jr., Old Westbury, New York.

Imp. Fairy Story

Owner: Mr. Stephen A. Sanford, Locust Valley, New York.

Aspiring Poloists

Place: Southern Arizona School for Boys, Tucson, Arizona.

Prompter, to Cart, and Trotter, Under Saddle
A World's Record, 2:01¾, for a mile

Equestrienne: Miss Joanne Link
Horses: Robin Hill Margene, Robin Hill Mam'zelle, and Topsy Turvy

Owner: Robin Hill Stables, Mr. and Mrs. Fred M. Link, Westwood, New Jersey.

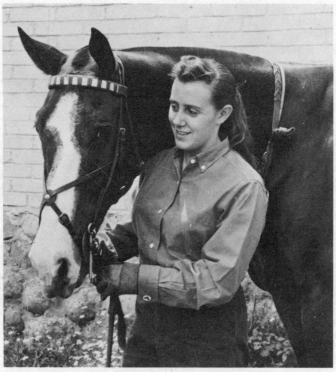

Equestrienne: Srta. Virginia Mariles y Valdes
Horse: Guerrerense

Owner: Brig. Gen. Humberto Mariles, Mexico City, Mexico.

Equestrienne: Miss Virginia Cronan
Horse: Kalarama Artist

Owner: Miss Virginia Cronan, Shamrock Farm, Louisville, Kentucky.

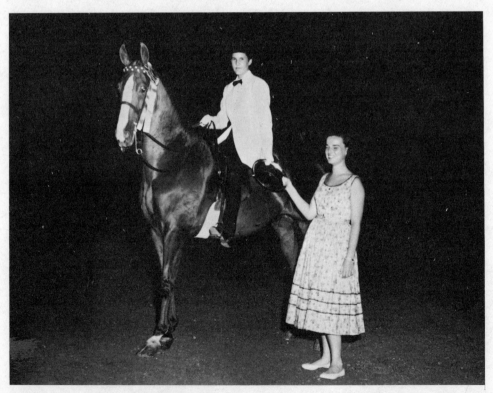

Equestrienne: Miss Judy Johnson
Horse: Sparkling Delight

Owner: Miss Judy Johnson, Castleton Farm, Lexington, Kentucky.

Equestrienne: Miss Rebecca Smyth
      Horse: Stardai

Owner: Jordan Arabian Farm, Mr. and Mrs. Edward B. Jordan, Fairport, New York.

Equestrian: Master James T. D'Arcy, Jr.
      Pony: Miles River Diamond

Owner: Welsh Valley Farms, Mr. James T. D'Arcy, Sr., Glen Moore, Pennsylvania.

The 1958 Equitation-Saddle Seat Winner of the American Horse Show Association, Medal Class Finals:

Equestrienne: Miss Lynne Girdler   Owner: Miss Lynne Girdler, Louisville, Kentucky.
                Horse: Storm Cloud

Various—Unusual

Whos Who? I Am! Mother Is Hoosier Honey

Watchin' and Waitin'

Steppin' High

Just Born

Just Restin'

Cattle Handling (Branding)

Barrel Racing

Runner and Trotter, Hitched Together

Prompter, Under Saddle, and Pacer, to Sulky. A New Jersey
Record, 2:01¼h for a mile

Runner, To Cart, A Pacer and A Trotter, To Sulkies

First Triple Dead Heat in Thoroughbred Racing,
Aqueduct Race Track, Aqueduct, New York.

First Triple Dead Heat in Harness Racing,
Freehold Raceway, Freehold, New Jersey.

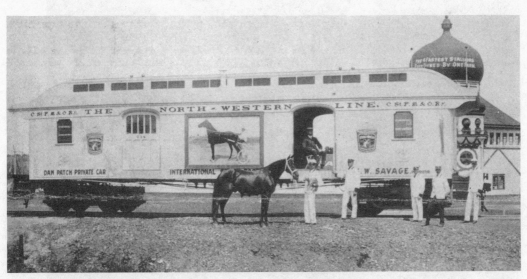

Dan Patch and His Private Railroad Pullman

Dan Patch, the Immortal Pacer, Earned Three Million Dollars Racing and Exhibiting.

Patoka, A Registered American Albino, and American Saddlebred

King Majesty, Pacer 2:10 h., A Multicolored Sire and
Abbe Yellow Brook and Foal (Colt)
Patricia Rosecroft and Foal (Filly)

Round Table Wins the United Nations Handicap

Tim Tam Wins the Florida Derby

Restless Wind Makes Like "a Gazelle"

Win, Place or Show (?)
    Hialeah Race Course, Hialeah, Florida.

Diamant, A German Holsteiner, High Jumper

Shoulder to Shoulder
Monmouth Park Jockey Club, Oceanport, New Jersey.

Ibn Rabdan, An Arab Stallion, Famous Progenitor
Sire: Rabban El Ajark   Dam: Bint Gameela

Cassandra, An Arab Mare, Famous Broodmare
Sire: Imp. Raffles   Dam: Rodetta

Daryan, An Arab
   Rider and Owner: Miss Donna West, Burlington, Wisconsin.

We Ride Arabians
   The Five Nelsons, Revere, Minnesota.

American Trotters: Mare and Suckling Twin Foals (Colts) at Walnut Hall Stud, Donerail, Kentucky.

French Trotters:
A Broodmare and Suckling Foal

Jamin, Stallion, Establishing an American Record of 1:58 4/5 for a Mile
Sire: Abner Dam: Dladys By: Hernahi III

Italian Trotters: Broodmares and Foals

Russian Orloff Trotters:
   A Broodmare and Weanling Foal

Russian Orloff Trotter:
   Otklik, Stallion
   Sire: Otboy   Dam: Katrina   By: Dukach

A Troika Hitch presented to Mr. Cyrus E. Eaton, Cleveland, Ohio, by Premier Nikita Khrushchev on behalf of the Union of Soviet Socialist Republics

Horses

Konus—"Cone" (Left)

Natourschik—"Nature Boy" (Center)

Otklik—"Response" (Right)

Driver: Vladimir Fomin

Austrian Lippizaners:
Getting Acquainted

Grazing on a Mountainside

Icelandic Horses:
   An Interlude near Stóng, with Peter B. Dirlam (American Traveler)

Grazing Near Mount Hofsjökull

Norwegian Duns (Fjörds): Mare and Weanling Foal

Eglington Hunt Team:
  Mr. Vernon G. Cardy, Ex. MFH, on Times Square
  Miss Helen Ferguson, Hon. Whip, on Maple Leaf
  Mrs. Vernon G. Cardy, Hon. Whip, on Gold Lode

A Coach and Four Hackney Horses, Transporting Racing Officials—
Santa Anita, California.

Sunsan, An Arab, Doing Tricks

Catoctin Gold (Goldie), A Palomino, A Finis Bow